No
Nice Girl
Swears

No Nice Girl Swears

NOTES ON HIGH SOCIETY, SOCIAL
GRACES, AND KEEPING YOUR WITS
FROM A JAZZ AGE DEBUTANTE

◆

ALICE-LEONE MOATS

Forewords by STELLENE VOLANDES, Editor In Chief of *Town & Country*,
and EDNA WOOLMAN CHASE, Former Editor in Chief of *Vogue*

APOLLO
PUBLISHERS

No Nice Girl Swears: Notes On High Society, Social Graces,
and Keeping Your Wits from a Jazz Age Debutante

No Nice Girl Swears was originally published in 1933.
New design and text © 2019 by Apollo Publishers.

Apollo Publishers books may be purchased for educational, business, or
sales promotional use. Special editions may be made available upon request.
For details, contact Apollo Publishers at info@apollopublishers.com.
Visit our website at www.apollopublishers.com.

Library of Congress Cataloging-in-Publication Data is available on file.

Print ISBN: 978-1-948062-42-8
Ebook ISBN: 978-1-948062-43-5

Printed in the United States of America.

To my mother and father

Contents

Preface • 9

Foreword by Stellene Volandes, *Town & Country* • 13

Foreword by Edna Woolman Chase, *Vogue* • 17

No Nice Girl Swears • 21

Should She Ask Him In? • 27

You're the First Man I've Ever Kissed • 31

Keeping an Amateur Standing • 37

This Casual Era • 41

May I Call You Up Some Time? • 45

Out for No Good • 51

Joining In • 55

Launching a Belle • 59

Chaperons Do Exist • 65

Between Courses • 69

The Inevitable Details • 73

Lunches and Teas; Or, Scarcely Worth the Trouble • 79

Coming Out to Music • 85

Cutting In and Sitting Out • 91

That Certain Something • 97

The Great Step • 99

In a Cloud of Tulle • 105

Twice Shy—? • 115

Travel Broadens the Mind • 119

Never Speak to Strangers Unless They Speak to You • 125

Out of Town • 133

Summer, Winter, Spring • 137

An Old English Custom • 143

In a Strange Bed • 153

Pity the Poor Working Girl • 159

Serious Business • 163

Hot Footlights • 167

The Hiccupping Fifties • 171

Our Plastered Friends • 177

Preface

———— ◆ ————

Originally published in 1933, *No Nice Girl Swears* was emblematic of a milestone moment in women's history and a turning point for social conventions. While debutante balls were still in full swing, Prohibition was on its last leg, and women were foraying into the workplace.

Reflecting back on *No Nice Girl Swears* fifty years after its original publication, Alice-Leone Moats, by then a world-traveling journalist, recounted the revolutionary nature of the book and the sensationalist headlines it received: "Young Society Girl Writes a Handbook in the Spirit of Modern Jazz Age; Etiquette for Taxicab Lovemaking Lists Ten Methods of Attack; New Volume Tells Debs How to Handle Drunks."

It was considered a defining book on the "new etiquette," lauded and celebrated by modern, forward-thinking women like Moats, arguably the feminists of their time, and by reviewers, but also met with disdain from those who preferred the more prim and proper conventions of days gone by.

Indeed, in addition to advice on fashion and the best way of dressing for all occasions, Moats dared to publicly advise on real issues that were often simply brushed under the table. Through wit and wisdom, she wrote candidly, though with earnest sass and a bit of satire occasionally thrown in, on topics such as how to handle a date who's had too much to drink, how to avoid unwanted advances, and how to prevent a boss from "taking liberties." While times have changed, this advice is certainly timeless. So, too, is advice on quality party throwing and personalized thank you notes, and her tips for style and grace, self-confidence, and putting your best foot forward.

If Moats's account of the circumstances surrounding the book's original publication was told with brutal honesty, the book was originally created at the behest of publishing legend—and husband to Amelia Earhart—George Palmer Putnam, who expected a more conservative guidebook. He proposed one ghost writer after another to Moats, until she claimed that she'd decided only a man could do the job and that she'd met one who had ghosted several best sellers, but would only assist under the condition that she would never share his name. Putnam agreed, and Moats pocketed the fee set for the ghost and wrote the book herself. On its completion, the book faced a range of challenges; it was dismissed by Putnam and passed between publishing houses as publishers and salespeople worried about the scandalous nature of the topics and advice featured inside. When at last it was released, it was a quick best seller.

Today, we live in a time when etiquette of any kind—even good manners—is under threat. The debates over whether chivalry is dead, or should even exist, seem hard to recall in a time when "locker room talk" is widely accepted. Perhaps we're even living in a culture that is "post–political correctness," where people believe we've come so far that we can reverse course and speak freely no matter how derogatory—or false—our statements may be. Certainty the internet, and particularly people's ability to write anonymously on it, has shaken the practice of good etiquette and manners to its core.

Our rerelease of Alice-Leone Moat's masterpiece, *No Nice Girl Swears*, comes at a time when looking at the history of etiquette presents an opportunity to consider where it's come from and where society would like it to be. There is also something enthralling in taking a much-needed respite from the chaos of today and delving into the glamour of the society life of days gone by. If the release also encourages a return to elegant afternoon dresses, chic, light-colored sports clothes, all-summer getaways, champagne-infused dinner parties, or perhaps even engraved invitations, well, all the better.

Julia Abramoff
Publisher
Apollo Publishers

Foreword by Stellene Volandes, Editor In Chief of *Town & Country*

To be perfectly honest, I hate the word "etiquette" and all the finger wagging, nose-in-the-air stuffiness, and outdated, prim rigidity it conjures. But this, my friends, is no etiquette book. No one would choose to sit next to an etiquette expert at dinner who might lecture on matters of cutlery and wine and water glasses and whether or not the invitation was indeed engraved. But for Alice-Leone Moats, you would gladly pull up a chair.

It's not that she doesn't address rules and standards in this book, first published in 1933. There are, to be clear, several chapters devoted to the details and decorum of the Deb Ball, but she does it all with equal doses of wit and wisdom and, most notably, common sense. Her guide is led not by a sense that one group of people knows what is right, but that we all should—if, that is, we would stop and think for a moment about how to treat each other and how we would like to be treated before we acted, or put off writing a thank you, or maybe accepted a dance card invitation. (And part of the fun of reading this—and there is plenty of fun—is when terms like "dance card" pop up. For some they will prove nostalgic; for others they might inspire a Google-search rabbit hole of bygone and often charming social mores.) One of my favorite moments is when Moats considers where ethics and etiquette collide. "It has grown increasingly confusing," she writes in the chapter titled "Should She Ask Him In?", "to determine where etiquette ends and ethics begin. . . . Just as good manners are a reflection of kindness and thoughtfulness, etiquette is the outgrowth of the combination of ethics and manners."

Throughout, though presented in an entertaining dinner-party-gossip tone with lively anecdotal evidence, the advice delivered here tackles this question and navigates its challenge. The guidance offered is not mired down by custom and tradition, but rather led by the reality of a time—1933, yes, but with an understanding that ensuing years would bring change and we should welcome it—and anchored in what she calls "an innate sense of the fitness of things, and sure feelings for the correct time and place." She asks our sense of civility to lead the way—as it should—with accommodations made for "slight romantic lapses" and even cigarettes on the dance floor.

All I wanted to do after reading this was run into Alice-Leone Moats one on one, and ask her what she thought about Twitter retweets and email condolence letters and Paperless Post wedding invitations. And of course about the title. If *No Nice Girl Swears*, then where does that leave me?

1933 Foreword by Edna Woolman Chase, Former Editor In Chief of *Vogue*

Etiquette has long been looked upon as a matter of custom and tradition, the residue of human experience. Built up from the manners of well-bred people, it has not—like fashion or literature—been subject to radical changes. A good etiquette book could be counted on as a permanent guide through the intricacies of social life. Once you mastered it, you were equipped for formal entrance into the world of convention.

But, unfortunately or otherwise, custom stales, and even the best tradition may become merely an old story. Manners are growing very nearly as fickle as modes, and they date you as unmistakably. Last year's etiquette, in fact, may be this year's humor: just a quaint old custom.

All this will seem heretic to the generation that learned painstakingly the exact number of cards to leave when calling on a married woman in whose house were living a widowed daughter and a maiden sister; and at just what moment it was permissible to remove one's white glacé kid gloves at a party. At least a few of the problems of the present day are, in truth, caused by the fact that so many women still wear white kid gloves mentally and try to clutter their children's lives with things as ineffectual as the scrolls in old-fashioned penmanship.

Even more recent generations may not approve of some of the advice offered in this book. We ourselves regret that it should be necessary to include rules for the treatment of a very sick escort who seemed quite up to the last three cocktails. Perhaps it isn't necessary in the very best circles—but who stays in the very best circles, or in any other circles, these days? Circles overlap like the shingles on a roof, and your most carefully guarded offspring is likely to find herself at a party with anyone from a bullfighter to Prince Mike himself—and should be forewarned accordingly.

This being the case, Miss Moats's guide to very modern etiquette seems to us an extremely useful little book. It does not ignore all the good old rules. It tells you that chaperons still do exist; that one still writes bread-and-butter letters and has certain obligations as a guest; that not even the current debutante gives expensive presents to her best beau; and that good manners are still nourished by the milk of human kindness.

It tells a great deal more, too, with a shrewdness of observation that few young women possess, and with a wit that makes entertaining reading. And so, if you are one of the not-so-very-young, we recommend that you read this book carefully as an aid in understanding what your daughter is up against.

Then, we suggest, pass it on to her as a chart to follow through these alarmingly changing times, when nothing that is not up-to-the-minute in any line seems really dependable.

No Nice Girl Swears

—— ◆ ——

Let's face it. Times and manners have changed so much and with such rapidity that the older generation can't even pause to be horrified and talk about the "old days." They're too breathless trying to keep up. This is essentially the day of youth. Nobody is too young any more to assume any position—from that of bank president to that of social arbiter. But neither is anyone too old—that is, if able to keep in the swing and stand the swift tempo.

The bars of age have disappeared, and the social ones have been let down so far as to be practically no impediment. It doesn't really matter where you were born. But if you haven't a great name, you must have some outstanding quality to distinguish you from the masses—talent, beauty, or even that superlative kind of stupidity that makes you a perfect listener, a person who can make up part of a background and be counted on to fill in empty corners. Everybody makes his own rules, for individuality has come into its own. The slogan of the age is: "Do as you please if you can get away with it."

As usual the little word if prefaces the meat of the sentence. A famous genius (and note that we say famous) can get away with anything, but the rest of us must conform to certain unalterable rules and regulations if we wish to be accepted socially. And, paradoxical as it may seem, this liberty of behavior requires more real breeding than ever. You must have an innate sense of the fitness of things, and sure feeling for the correct time and place.

Nothing could better illustrate today's "Who cares?" attitude towards the amenities of the drawing-room than the careless positions we assume in chairs, on sofas, and even on the floor. Except under the most unusual circumstances nobody ever bothers to sit up in a chair. At least one foot is always tucked under the sitter, when both aren't propped up on something. Even schools have given up the useless fight of making their pupils sit up like little ladies. The most elaborate

India-rubber twistings have come to look quite natural, and even the primmest are no longer startled by this nonchalance. But it also serves to illustrate the sentence about doing as you please if you can get away with it. By all means, sit in any position you like, so long as you have pretty legs.

Nowadays a woman smokes at any time or in any place. There are a few men left who wax sentimental when a girl says she doesn't smoke, but even they automatically go on offering her cigarettes. It's just smug to say: "No, I don't smoke," when confronted with a cigarette-case. "No, thank you," is quite sufficient. But it's still not the thing for a woman to smoke on the street, except that, although for a long time no real lady puffed on a cigarette in a car or a taxi, she now does it with the nonchalance she would display in her own drawing-room. The dance floor is the one place where it is unforgivable for either a woman or a man to carry a lighted cigarette. This last, however, has nothing to do with etiquette—it's merely a measure of safety, for it is too simple to ignite your partner (don't misunderstand) or set a diaphanous dress ablaze.

A similar change of attitude has come about towards make-up. Gone are the days of the surreptitious rouge-pot. Even young girls recognize the importance of taking care of their skins, and dressing-tables are quite frankly littered with bottles and jars. As regards cosmetics, the only sin against society seems to be make-up badly applied. The "Would you brush your teeth in public?" attitude towards make-up died quietly some time ago. Even the most jaundiced dowager will admit that powder-puffs and the unrestrained use of a lipstick outside the boudoir are certainly preferable to trailing round shiny-nosed and pale-lipped.

The same lack of restraint found in posture, make-up, and smoking is evident in conversation. There is scarcely a subject left which is considered too delicate to discuss in the draw-ing-room or that awesome thing of the nineties, mixed com-pany. Any topic is introduced quite casually. The only object is to make one's meaning clear. Words which our grandmothers knew only because they were assiduous Bible-readers are in such current use that it comes as a distinct surprise to find anyone who is shocked by them. It was only a few years ago that audiences gasped or tittered self-consciously at a play in which any of a number of little English phrases known the world over were used. Now even the censors have given up. Of course, in any period, it is wise to have a little geographical discretion; adapt your conversation to your surroundings. It is pretty crude to set out deliberately to horrify people. And if you are a lily or sweet and girlish, stick to your type and mind your conversation. You haven't a chance. Coming from you, any remark, be it ever so slightly off color, will sound raw.

Mrs. Post tells us that no lady ever uses slang or swears. Surely this is a slight exaggeration. Or have we been misled by the novels of her day in which the heroines, perfect little ladies all, would in moments of girlish daring refer to their chaperons as "gooseberries," talk of "spooning" (although heaven forfend they should have practiced it) and use "daisy" where we use "swell"? Whatever expressions happen to be the current style in slang fall into such general use that the most sensitive ear becomes accustomed to them, and stubborn purists end by adopting them unconsciously (usually, it is true, after the rest of the world has had to find something new or go mad). But swearing is slightly different. It has not been affected by vogues, and although an occasional "damn" passes unnoticed, any systematic swearing on the part of a woman comes as a shock. It is always ugly and particularly, in moments of stress, vulgar. People who preface every sentence with "My God" are worse. They're tiresome.

Should She
Ask Him In?

———— ◆ ————

It has grown increasingly confusing to determine where etiquette ends and ethics begin, and the fact that nobody quite knows the exact meaning of ethics only adds to the general confusion. Just as good manners are a reflection of kindness and thoughtfulness, etiquette is the outgrowth of the combination of ethics and manners.

The famous slogan "Should she ask him in?" is one of the best examples of the way etiquette and ethics merge into each other. And it all really comes down to what you mean by asking a man in. A girl who lives with her family has no reason to hesitate on doorsteps at night. Be it seven in the evening or four in the morning, her escort may march in for a drink or something to eat, safe in the knowledge that the family, awake or asleep, is always sufficient chaperon.

The working girl or the girl who for some other reason lives alone is the one with the real problem to solve. Here are three rules that might prove helpful: Set the time limit at midnight; make sure the gentleman is sober; know your man—it is plain foolhardiness to ask a casual acquaintance in.

Knowing your man is easier said than done, for it appears difficult for masculine mentality to grasp the difference between living alone and living loosely. Too often men overlook the fact that a woman in business earns her money in an office.

The other side of the question is why and when a girl goes to a man's apartment. It is nothing short of excessive prudery for someone who has been out one or two years to refuse to dine in a bachelor flat, either alone or in a party. The very timid may consider an extra man as sufficient chaperon. Not only will you get better food, but you can scarcely demand, that a man who has a running household pay for a dinner in a restaurant merely in order to save your priceless reputation. Anyway, consideration for a young man's pocket-book always helps your popularity along. If you feel that he is not to be trusted in his own house, you might as well cut him off your list, as he can make just as many opportunities in a taxi or other vehicle. We return to the question of the hour. Follow in Cinderella's footsteps and go home early.

The key to the whole situation lies in the fact that you don't know when or by whom you will be seen coming in or going out. The most harmless visit can assume a naughty appearance, and certainly an acquaintance seeing you come out of a man's apartment in the early hours just before dawn will draw but one conclusion. Avoid stopping in for a drink after the theater, as the hour is a bit late, and it gives the young man ideas. Don't fall for the old line of having to go home for a long-distance call, and at the very mention of works of art run in the opposite direction. In any event, an innocent visit late at night seems rather silly, for it is taking a maximum risk for a minimum pleasure.

You're the First Man
I've Ever Kissed

———— ◆ ————

There seems to be a feeling that petting has a place in a book of modern manners, although we cannot understand, why the idea should be current that this sport belongs only to the present generation. Call it spooning or call it necking, it's still petting to us. Again referring to Mrs. Post, we note that this practice "has no more place in distinguished society than any other actions that are cheap, promiscuous, or vulgar." A sweeping statement, to say the least! If this august lady's rule were to be followed when separating the sheep from the goats, society would soon dwindle to well below the magical "four hundred." And where would we be at that rate? But here we are, back again at the subtle nuances with which petting is more fraught than any other pastime. The real difference lies between promiscuity (that is, petting for petting's sake) and slight romantic lapses.

Anyone will admit that in the long run a reputation for being a heavy necker doesn't really add to a girl's popularity. She will undoubtedly be a belle, but only a flash in the pan, for no matter how much skill is displayed, it is pretty difficult to keep a beau for any length of time by playing this hazardous game. You can't hope to get away with the "You're the first man I've ever kissed" line with seventeen different men. The day will inevitably come when your name will be brought up over a bottle of brandy, and your talents discussed. Remember, after the first few drinks gallantry is likely to get lost in the general fog. But, after all, this whole business is a very personal problem and one you can scarcely expect someone else to work out for you.

In this day of the waning chaperon it requires real dexterity to keep a man on the string and yet never let him get an opportunity to make a direct pass. Often you would like him as a beau, but not as a lover. If you ever give a man a chance to declare his intentions, honorable or otherwise, in words or by pantomime, your friendship is over and you have only two alternatives—to take him up on it or to refuse him. Of course a man will not go on forever in the role of potential lover, but if you are clever, you can gain time by seeing to it that he never has a real opportunity to explain his feelings. Avoid romantic atmosphere—moonlit gardens, deserted beaches, and evenings alone in front of a fire. Without being too deliberate, you can see to it that you are never alone with him for any great length of time. In a taxicab you can talk on brightly and innocently, for nothing puts a man off like conversation, and when all else fails, there is always a cigarette.

The technique of warding off passes is one which every girl should perfect. Not but what she gets all the necessary opportunity, as there is something about the atmosphere of a taxi-cab that makes the most indifferent male grow ardent. There are two kinds of passes: the verbal and the physical. The first can be easily overlooked, as it need never be understood; but the second, alas, is always too clear to admit of any misunderstanding. Direct measures are required, and it is not always easy to escape a gentleman's too pressing attentions with tact as well as firmness. Evasiveness and flippancy are the best weapons—if they work. Of course, if you never wish to see the man again, you can use the direct rebuff, or the kicking and screaming method. But even that fails if you happen to draw a rough-and-tumble type. If you can get away with the "Sir, you've insulted me" attitude, by all means adopt it. We never could.

It is no longer taken for granted that a girl who is seen out with a married man is "carrying on" with him. If she makes a habit of going out constantly with another woman's husband, it will naturally cause talk, although in these days of easy divorce one cannot jump to the conclusion that the gentleman's intentions aren't honorable. It often happens that for some reason a man will take out his wife's best friend. In fact, it has become quite an accepted practice. If the wife doesn't object, no one else has the right to do so. When you dine or lunch with a married man, however, our advice would be to insist upon a well-known restaurant, for if you go to a small, obscure place, you give a furtive, clandestine air to the whole thing. But in spite of appearances or a wife's real or apparent approval it is just as well to avoid going out too often with an attached male unless you have absolute confidence in your own ability to keep the situation in hand. He will require more dexterous handling than a bachelor, for he feels entirely too safe and is all for making use of his rare moments of freedom.

When all is said and done, discretion is what counts. It is the girl who just must tell on herself who gets into trouble. Often she will be far more innocent than the quiet, subtle type who does pretty much as she pleases, but knows how to keep quiet about it. Of course it seems all wrong that in this world appearances count for more than actions, but it has always been so and we can do nothing but accept it. Even those of us who most dislike hypocrisy have to think of the looks of the thing.

No matter how many times you have been to a man's house, always act as if it were a first visit. Remarks such as: "Do the new curtains in your room keep out the light?" or: "Oh, look, the sofa now faces the window," imply a greater intimacy than might exist and are never appreciated by the host. More women give themselves away from vanity than from carelessness. Don't let your vanity get the better of your common sense. Anyway, it's good technique to be discreet.

Keeping an
Amateur Standing

— ◆ —

Flowers, books, and candy are considered the only presents which a lady may accept from a man. A jeweled bangle or some similar gift of trifling value may be received without fear of criticism, but expensive jewelry and wearing-apparel of any kind mean but one thing to this cynical world. There is only one way to pay for these, and few girls are so charming and lovely that they can forever defy the laws of economics and get something for nothing.

Don't get reckless over the gifts you make to your best beau. Cigarette-cases and other expensive items are more or less taken for granted when you are engaged—that is, if you have the necessary means. At other times it is not only in bad taste to shower diamond cuff-links and pearl studs on a young man, but intensely embarrassing to him. Let yourself go at Christmas and birthdays on old friends, but even then curb your generosity and pick out things like money-clips, bill-folds, or good-luck medals. Of course, there are always photographs. Every beau eventually feels called upon to ask for one. When you reach this inevitable point, think well before producing your most recent likeness. It is quite easy not to have one on hand at the moment. Sad as it may seem, unless you intend to marry the man, the time will surely come when you will ask that he return your picture, immediately lending unnecessary emphasis to the whole episode.

Under no circumstances scrawl any of those "Forever thine" sentiments across a photograph. "To my darling Rollo, lest you forget," is not only indiscreet, but out and out wet. Whether the picture is intended for a man or a woman, follow the example set by royalty and simply sign your name. Celebrities are the only exception to this rule. It is more gracious for them to write something above their signature, if only the recipient's name, as: "To Richard Halliburton— Lydia E. Pinkham."

Effusions of any kind have gone completely out of style,

and nowhere is this more true than in letter-writing. When your latest beau goes to South America, don't try to out-Ethel Miss Dell and go off into passionate flights of literary ecstasy in an attempt to describe emotions which no one human is capable of feeling. If you can't restrain yourself, at least extract a promise from your correspondent that he will tear the letters up as soon as they are read. And make this a rule with those you yourself receive. Packages of love-letters tied up in pastel ribbons smack ridiculously of the nineties, and if you are a newspaper-reader, we need scarcely warn you of the trouble and embarrassment they can cause.

This Casual Era

———— ◆ ————

In no way is the offhand attitude of these days as apparent as in the extravagant use of Christian names. Even at a first meeting girls who belong to the same set never "Miss" each other, and most younger married women soon fall into the more familiar form. It's slightly different when both sexes are involved. Ordinarily a young man and a girl use Christian names shortly after they've met, but it's up to the girl to take the initiative. It is impossible to give the correct length of time which should elapse before switching from "Mr. Tarbel" to "Joseph." Rely on your woman's intuition. During that uncertain period use "You." Of course, all this is true only between people of the same age. You can scarcely go around calling your grandfather's best friend "Aloysius." He will undoubtedly call you by your given name. So will—and, for that matter, so should—the parents of your friends.

Never, never, never refer to your husband or wife as "Mr." or "Mrs." when you are speaking to friends. This is a form entirely reserved for servants and employees, to whom you say: "Please tell Mr. Lamb that Bromo-Seltzer is what he needs," or: "Did Miss Eufemia come in last night?" For social usage "my husband" or "Jules" are the only possibilities, and there isn't much choice, as the first is for acquaintances, and the second for friends. If you simply can't keep from talking about your children, remember to use only their Christian names.

We go right on using the old forms of introduction in spite of the fact that practically no one bothers to listen to a name when introduced. The first name mentioned is determined by the sex, age, or importance of the person, the theory being that the smaller fry is presented to the greater. If you must be formal, you may say: "Mrs. Stone, may I present Mr. Flint?" But the more current form is merely: "Mrs. Stone—Mr. Flint." Your own friends are just "Mary Vernon" or "Jack Hill" when you are introducing them to your parents. "How do you do?" in the way of acknowledgment is sufficient for any occasion. "Charmed," "Pleased to meet you," and similar remarks are terrible—never to be used under any circumstances. Do as you like about shaking hands, but it is certainly more friendly than bowing stiffly. If you're the kind who can't resist adding that little intimate touch, your chance will come at parting, when you can say: "It has been a great pleasure to meet you." If you should happen to be the victim of this sally, "Thank you," or "The pleasure has been mine" will do nicely. A hostess is expected to see that all her guests meet each other, but if you should happen to be overlooked, go right ahead and talk to anyone you please. The very fact that you are under a friend's roof constitutes an introduction. All this casualness is beginning to show even in the outward, relations of married couples. In the last few years Americans have taken to sophistication with the energy they show in everything, so when incompatibility crops up in the home, a couple are more apt to be continental and go their separate ways quite amicably rather than taking a dusty train-ride to Reno. There are many couples who go out of their way to keep their friends and engagements separate. And if that's the way they feel about it, the rest of the world has no choice but to respect their attitude.

Therefore the question of inviting husbands and wives separately is one which arises very frequently. For all large dinners or balls the invitations must invariably read: "Mr. and Mrs."; otherwise it all depends on the people themselves. However, don't make the mistake of inviting a husband without his wife unless you are pretty sure that they've adopted this modern behavior. Strangely enough, it's a less serious *faux pas* to ask a wife without her husband, although again it all depends upon the individual. Of course, in a pinch you can always borrow your best friend's husband (or wife, as the case may be)—that is, if you're sure your intentions won't be misunderstood.

May I Call You
Up Some Time?

———— ◆ ————

Engraved invitations are now seldom used, except for coming-out parties, very formal dinners, and balls. They are seen almost as seldom as visiting-cards, which have only two uses: to mark the doorbell of a walk-up apartment and to send with flowers and gifts. One never pays formal calls any more. It's sheer nonsense for us to go into the matter of the size, engraving, and other details of invitations and visiting-cards. Take your troubles to an expert stationer or jeweler, like Mauboussin, who keeps abreast of the times.

The telephone is used for practically everything. Dates that aren't made by that convenient means are arranged by word of mouth, notes, and telegrams. It's all done in an offhand way, and it isn't even considered necessary to know a person well before accepting an invitation.

It is quite proper to meet a young man at a cocktail party and go on to dinner with him. If he is attractive, you can consider yourself not only correct, but lucky. Of course before accepting an invitation from a complete stranger it is wise to look him over and decide whether or not you will be willing to have him around in the future. There is no sense in taking a chance on a bore, as, once annexed, he will be hard to lose. It is sad but true that the more amusing the young man, the less apt he is to telephone a girl after their first meeting. For some reason the dull are always bolder. With the persistent type who mentions all seven days in the week after you have refused him a date it is better not to be kind-hearted. Be firm from the first, as eventually you will be forced into rudeness in order to get rid of him. The sooner you get it over with, the better.

"May I call you up some time?" is a sentence that may signify anything. It is sometimes difficult to know whether a man really means it or whether he is merely making conversation. The warmth of your reply often has much to do with turning an idle remark into a definite intention. If you do want to hear from him, you needn't fall on his neck with loud cries of joy; you can reply: "Please do" with a warm look (but you probably know much more about that than we do), adding: "I'm in the telephone directory" or whatever other means there is of reaching you. If you are living at home and have the kind of parents who don't mind unexpected callers, you can suggest that he drop in some afternoon or evening for a drink.

You have a chance to show your ingenuity when you meet an attractive man whom you would really like to see again. Although it is considered very natural and flattering for a man to attempt to see a girl again after one meeting, it is "forward" of her to take the initiative. The good old feminine stand-by—the roundabout attack—is the only possible one to use in such a predicament. If by chance you are giving a dinner, dance, or cocktail party, the matter is comparatively simple. The handsome stranger can scarcely think you are pursuing him when he is merely one of twenty other guests. If you fear the impression you made was so slight that he won't remember your name, don't telephone. A note with an allusion to the person at whose house you met is less embarrassing. In your enthusiasm don't call him by his Christian name. He is "Dear Mr. Armstrong" to you.

It was once unheard-of for a young lady to accept an invitation from a gentleman whom her family had never met. Now it's all left to chance and you are not expected to make elaborate arrangements for presenting Basil to Mamma. A modern mother is not one to insist upon knowing what intentions the young man entertains towards her daughter. It's probably just as well for her peace of mind.

Going to the house of a person whom you have never met is something which should not be undertaken too lightly. The one time you need have no hesitation about being taken to a stranger's house is for a cocktail party. These affairs are always informal and require so little planning that an extra person or two makes no difference. But for any other occasion it is never safe to go to a house uninvited unless you can rely absolutely upon the person who takes you. You needn't, of course, demand an engraved invitation, but you should insist upon having the hostess write a note or telephone you. A woman is always more conscientious than a man about these matters, so with a feminine guide you are spared that apprehensive feeling that there won't be an extra place at table. Except in unusual circumstances, there is something very uncomfortable about being taken to a stranger's house by a man. It immediately puts you in an ambiguous position. The hostess sometimes doesn't understand, and it's taken for granted that you and your escort have a little too much in common.

While we're on the subject of dates, we might as well go into the "blind" variety. It is not good form or lack of it that should worry you in accepting a blind date—it's the risk you run of being bored to death.

There are two kinds of blind dates. The first: George has a friend, Joe Gutch, who either is a stranger in town or, for some reason, knows no girls. Kind-hearted George asks Helen to provide another girl for the occasion, and the merry foursome sets forth. All too soon the poor girl discovers that the probable reason why somebody had to be provided for Joe is that he, on his own, couldn't possibly get anything but a blind deaf-mute. The second: George arranges a date for his good friend Henry with Mary, and they go out alone together. Unless Mary knows that George's taste in men is infallible, she had better take our advice and plead another engagement. And she will do well to keep in mind that one man's opinion of another is usually founded upon whether he was once able to drink the entire University of Virginia under the table (an impossible feat, we understand) or is a good football-player. Undoubtedly worthy qualities, but of little use to a girl.

Out for No Good

———— ◆ ————

Making an official debut is one of the few antiquated social customs that we cling to. That is to say, the custom has remained, though its significance has long since been forgotten.

The original idea was to keep a girl in the background until she reached the age of eighteen. Then she learned to swish a train, twisted her hair into a Langtry knot, or whatever happened to be the current fashion, and was presented to society by her mother, which meant that she was presented to her mother's friends and all the eligible young men available, who, with the exception of relatives and a few family intimates, had never seen her before.

A coming-out ball or dinner was given in the girl's home, and thereafter she accompanied her parents to all the social functions of the season and made her appearance in the family box on the first night of the opera. She was officially "out," had been introduced to the best society, and was ready for marriage, and the parents took good care to see that she met no ineligibles.

It is a far cry from those days of the watchful mamma and the restricted parties to these, when a mother and daughter seldom meet and never go to the same parties; when any man is invited to a coming-out ball so long as he is young and not too crippled to stand in the stag line.

Now only a few older people, friends of the debutante's family, are invited to her coming out, and the rest of the guests are the other debutantes of the season and hundreds of young men recruited from the lists of social secretaries. If she is a person of assured social position and knows her guests personally, they are likely to be boys and girls she has known since dancing-school days, so that one can hardly say she is being "introduced" to society.

Every year there are a few serious-minded young ladies who feel the urge to go to college and get full of education, but nevertheless want to make a debut. This seemingly impossible feat is accomplished by returning home over the week-ends so that they can take in all the Saturday dances and many Friday ones as well. They have their own party either during the vacation or over one of the week-ends. It is a rather hectic business, and it seems to us that a girl should make up her mind what her type is going to be. It seems silly to put blue stockings on a butterfly.

Sometimes, owing to limited means, mourning, or illness in the family, a girl will come out without giving a party. But this is a luxury which only a person of secure social standing can permit herself, for in this case she must depend upon a large circle of friends who will invite her to all their debuts, as well as an unlimited male acquaintance who will see that she has a good time. Whatever form a coming out takes, a debutante needs pretty clothes and rates an outfit that can almost be compared to a bride's trousseau. She should have at least five evening dresses, all formal, for she needs no "in-betweens" that year. Her clothes should be smart, but not too sophisticated, and certainly not too naked. Modest dresses are undoubtedly in far better taste for young girls. They needn't have cap sleeves or bits of tulle tied about the neck, but a happy medium can always be reached without destroying their chic.

Debutantes have a passion for wearing black—a tendency which should be curbed by the mother, as it is old and usually unbecoming. White and gay colors are the best for all occasions. On the night of her coming-out party it is customary for the debutante to wear a white dress, although there is no fixed rule for this. Usually the frock is one which has not been worn before, but of course if the party is in January and she cannot afford to buy a new one so late in the season, her best evening dress will do.

A winter coat with a fur collar or a fur coat; two dresses to wear under it, one for morning and lunching, one slightly more formal for tea dancing; two hats; and all the necessary accessories—this is the minimum, but quite sufficient for town. Of course the girl with wealthy parents need have no limit to her wardrobe.

Enormous solitaire rings, diamond bracelets three inches wide, long ear-rings, whether real or imitation, and imposing brooches are all in atrocious taste for a girl of eighteen—in fact, for any young unmarried girl. Parents often give their daughters some jewel for a coming-out present, although heaven knows why this should be added to their already excessive burden of expense.

Joining In

—— ◆ ——

Making a formal debut isn't so simple as one would think. A poor mother has to begin making plans for her daughter's coming out long before it actually takes place. For instance, there are the Metropolitan and Colony dances to which she must go as a sub-debutante and which simplify her getting into the Junior Assemblies as a debutante. A year before the debut is the time to begin worrying about these salt subscription dances. The mother has to find out the names of the patronesses and write a letter making her request. If she isn't very well known, it might be better to ask for one or two letters seconding the girl.

There are three Junior Assembly dances every year, which

take place in the ballroom of the Ritz in December, January, and February. Under ordinary circumstances, a girl who is accepted goes to all of them the year she comes out and her second season as well. However, it occasionally happens that someone who is too important to be left out sends in her application late. When this occurs and the list is complete, the patronesses stretch a point and invite her for one of the dances. Lately the Assemblies have grown so large that the mothers of the girls attend only the first year, not the second. Some mothers dance, but most of them content themselves with sitting in the balcony and looking on.

Each girl invites two young men as escorts. Several dinners are invariably given to precede the dance, and with her acceptance of a dinner invitation a girl sends in the names of the two men to her hostess who, for once, hasn't the worry of collecting men for her dinner.

The girls are supposed to wear long white gloves, and the men also are expected to appear with hands carefully encased in white kid. This is the only time, we might add, that men wear gloves, although for the sake of our frocks we wish it would happen more often. All the patronesses stand at the head of the stairs and receive, and after that the affair goes on just like any other ball in New York, with these exceptions: no intoxicating drinks are served, "Home, Sweet Home" is played at two o'clock sharp, and it is obligatory for a girl to have supper with at least one of her escorts.

The Assemblies are extremely strict and exclusive. A girl must be "somebody" to get in—have some background and come of a well-known family. For that reason debutantes are anxious to belong, as it stamps them socially. It is one evening when every little deb should mind her p's and q's. If she never behaved well before, she must do so then, for she is being closely watched by the older members of New York's best. She should avoid any dancing postures which these elderly onlookers might consider vulgar and improper, and even her dress should be selected with care as to décolletage.

Then there is the Junior League, although in New York it is not so indispensable to a debutante's social career as it is in other cities. A girl who is not a real New Yorker should join the League, however, as it offers an unparalleled opportunity to meet other debutantes of the season and gives the person with a passion for charity work or with a clubwoman's nature a perfect chance to express herself. And the swimming-pool, indoor squash-courts, and other facilities for exercise help the harassed belle to keep her health during a strenuous first season.

In order to join, you must find five friends to help you; one to propose you, one to second you, and three to write letters of recommendation to the committee. If your name is accepted, you are on probation for the first year, during which time you take a six-weeks course of study in social welfare work. Then you are given a written examination on the subject, and only after passing it do you become a full-fledged member of the League.

Launching a Belle

———— ◆ ————

To many people it seems impossible that some parents actually engage press agents for their daughters the year they come out. The press agent, for a set sum, agrees to see that his client's photograph is in all the papers and fashionable magazines, that accounts of her activities are published continually, and that she is described as the prettiest, or the smartest, or the something-or-otherest debutante of the season. The extent of the superlatives probably depends upon the amount subscribed. Needless to say, only people very far outside the social pale would dream of doing anything in such atrocious taste. Only climbers court publicity.

Avoiding publicity is not so easy, however. A debutante

of any prominence has her life made miserable by photographers' secretaries with personality-plus voices. These creatures apparently telephone to hundreds of people every day. They even have the temerity to ring early in the morning when they know that a debutante never gets to bed before four or five, and it is not unusual for a girl to receive twenty calls of this kind between nine and one. "I am speaking for Mr. Leopold Levitsky," comes over the wire in saccharine tones; "he would so much like to take your photograph for publication in several magazines. Couldn't you give us an appointment? Of course you understand that you are under no obligation."

But just try going to one and refusing to buy any of the pictures! Nothing discourages them. Say you are leaving town for two months; they will call you at the end of that time; say you are too busy that week; they will call you the next; and so on. Politeness is of no avail; the only possible way of getting rid of one is to be downright rude. "I do not want my photograph taken today, tomorrow, or ever," will sometimes make your attitude clear.

A woman who is too busy to attend to the details of her daughter's coming-out party, or one who lacks the social backing to do so, can turn to a social agency for assistance.

There are several of these, and they will arrange all the details of a party. They make up the lists of guests, write out and mail invitations, engage the ballroom, plan the dinner or supper menus, attend to the decorations, and place somebody at the entrance to check off the guests as they arrive. And the results are as stereotyped and lacking in imagination as you would expect from a social Sears Roebuck.

For the new-rich and strangers in a city, social agencies are invaluable, since they invite all the people the hosts don't know. It is they who are greatly responsible for the splurging parties, swarming with unknown youths, for they figure that the larger and more elaborate the party, the greater their commissions. There still remain a few conservative hostesses who insist upon knowing all their guests, but even many of the better people have given in to inviting strangers to their parties, as they are assured that no dance is successful unless the men outnumber the girls by at least three to one.

They have their lists, A, B, and C. If a client is considered worthy, invitations are sent to the girls and men on A, most of whom won't accept if they don't know the hostess. Then the ones on B list are invited, and if most of them refuse, C is resorted to. The agencies will put themselves out for a debutante who is going to have a large, expensive party, no matter what her social status is, and will see that she gets invited to every entertainment which they arrange. On the other hand, the girl who spends little money is accorded far less attention, and the one who spends none is likely to be overlooked entirely, unless her name lends such luster to a list of guests that she heads it.

That discourtesy, the list at the door, is another result of inviting unknown people through social agencies. At coming-out balls a woman is seated at a little table in the entrance to check off the names of the guests as they file past. It can happen that through some mistake the name of a person who has been invited will be left off the list. If this happens to you, don't grow embarrassed and depart; send word to your hostess that you are downstairs, but are not allowed in. She will then dispatch an usher for you or come herself.

The system arose to prevent "crashing," which was so prevalent several years ago. It seems that it is a necessity for it is very difficult to tell the difference between one group of terrible-looking strange young men who happen to have been invited and another group who haven't. To the guests who are friends of the hostess, having to be checked off before being allowed to enter is a perpetual source of irritation and annoyance. It makes them feel very much as criminals must at a line-up. Surely, something better could be thought out. If each person presented his invitation at the door, it would be just as effective and far less ignominious. And, let us add, if only friends and acquaintances were invited, it would be fairly easy for a hostess to notice any stray crashers.

Chaperons Do Exist

———— ◆ ————

In spite of all the talk and writing to the contrary, chaperons still exist, and there are certain rules to which a deb should adhere unless she is the kind who just must be talked about. Each year finds hundreds of girls making their bows to New York society, but there are never more than twenty or thirty who have any just claim to social distinction. These are the ones who verge on the conservative and are always carefully chaperoned and it is they who set the pace for the social climbers.

The chaperon of today bears no resemblance to the eagle-eyed terror of yesterday. Whether a relative or a duenna hired for the job, she is ordinarily good-natured, half-blind, and extremely tolerant. She doesn't ask questions, is willing to stay where she is left, and doesn't obtrude her presence any more than necessary. She may have lost her authority, but she is still an indispensable figure-head. Few girls object to having a chaperon, for they realize that she actually supplies more freedom than she takes away. Her presence makes it difficult to gossip about a girl, no matter what happens. Just as a woman may do as she pleases without fear of ostracism so long as her husband is willing to play blind, a young girl may take all the liberties she likes if she remains under the aegis of a chaperon.

At every debutante ball, from one o'clock on, the entrance hall is lined with sleepy females all waiting patiently for their charges to get tired enough to leave the party. No girl in her first year out may go home unaccompanied by some older person. A maid who is willing to perform this service will do nicely, but usually it is an old governess or someone supplied by an agency which makes a specialty of respectable ladies.

Sometimes when there are several balls on the same evening, the guests will go from one to another. In any event, before going home the debutantes return to the first dance to pick up their chaperons.

At the age of eighteen, after two years spent as a sub-debutante, strictly watched and carefully nurtured, when going out alone with a man was out of the question, and restaurants were entered only with parents or friends of the family, a girl at last has a chance to go to public places with a more thrilling escort. But even then it can scarcely be called seeing life in a big way. It's quite proper for a debutante to lunch, tea-dance, and go to the movies or theater with any one of her beaux. She may even dine with one *tête à tête*, but only in a place which caters exclusively to a clientele of her friends. Even then it's considered more correct to be in a party of four. The ultra-fashionable restaurants are closed to her, as well as the type in which she is likely to run into Uncle Hiram with his latest blonde—little debs aren't supposed to know how to carry off a situation of this kind.

Lately an entirely new class of after-theater dancing-places has appeared, in the east-side residential section of New York. We continue to designate them as night clubs, although they have very little in common with the Broadway haunts which also bear that name. The former are purely social—there is nothing even slightly hot-cha about the entertainment or patrons. These are the ones which must satisfy debutantes who are in a devilish mood and want to step out. They may go in a party, if by any chance they haven't a big dance to go to, which seldom happens during the season. Speakeasies, even with a large group, are strictly taboo.

Debutantes are no exception to the rule that a woman smokes when, where, and as much as she pleases, but her drinking activities are somewhat more limited. Champagne at dinner is as far as her alcoholic dissipation goes. Cocktails and other hard liquor are out. One always hears much about the heavy drinking done by debutantes, but actually, when one learns the facts, it is never the girls of good families who pass out behind potted palms. This type of "bud" is one of those hybrids who think that by calling themselves debutantes they have achieved social distinction, although it is rather puzzling to know what they come out to.

Between Courses

———— ◆ ————

Now we come to the actual debut, which takes place any time between the first of October and the fifteenth of January. There are a number of ways of making an official bow to society, and for your edification we will take each one up in detail.

A dinner is a recognized way of coming out and, next to a ball, the most impressive. The guests may number anywhere from thirty to three hundred, but a dinner is supposed to be for at least fifty people. If it doesn't take place in a private house, a dining-room or balcony of a restaurant will do nicely. The object is not to mix with the regular patrons. By all means select a place with a dance orchestra, so that the young things can dance after each course. Heavy dinner conversation has not yet become their forte, and they had rather come back to a cold entrée than worry their little heads about the merits of Picasso.

Invitations to the dinner should be sent out at least four or six weeks in advance. As in the case of visiting-cards, any well-known jeweler can give you the necessary form to be engraved on the white cardboard squares. At all times those forms with a space left for the guest's name to be written in by hand are more correct for dinners. For a very large and formal dinner it is customary to use the following wording:

*Mr. and Mrs. Cadwallader Gerald Crest request the
pleasure of company at dinner in honor of their daughter
Miss Octavia Crest on Friday, December thirty-first at
eight o'clock*

R.S.V.P.

Jean's Dancing

Thirteen East Seventieth Street

For a smaller dinner (less than fifty):

*Mr. and Mrs. Cadwallader Gerald Crest request the
pleasure of company on Friday, December thirty-first at
eight o'clock*

Two Hundred and Fifty Park Avenue

R.S.V.P.

"To meet Miss Octavia Crest" written in the upper left-hand corner indicates that the party is given in that young lady's honor, and that she is a debutante.

An acceptance is written in the third person and carefully spaced, as:

For a refusal the form is similar, except that "owing to a previous engagement, is unable to accept" takes the place of "accepts with pleasure."

Miss Lily Blank
accepts with pleasure
Mr. and Mrs. Cadwallader Gerald Crest's
kind invitation for dinner
on Friday, December thirty-first
at eight o'clock at Jean's.

It is all very well to say that invitations should receive a prompt reply, but, as a rule, a New York hostess is in a panic a few days before her party. She invariably discovers that acceptances come in averaging about eight girls to one man—a sad state at any point in the game. What occurs is that the youths hoard their invitations and don't answer them until a day or two beforehand, when they have made certain where all their friends are going. This is just another of the evils of inviting people you don't know. And you certainly can't blame them for feeling no obligation towards a Mrs. Cadwallader Gerald Crest whom they have never seen in their lives.

The Inevitable Details

——— ◆ ———

As long as you are going to give a dinner party, you might as well take some trouble over ordering the food. If you leave it to the head waiter, he will give you the same menu that has been served at coming-out dinners from time immemorial. We can remember growing pale at the sight of the same pseudo filet of sole with tired grapes, and ice cream with chocolate sauce and cherries, which appeared with nauseating regularity at any dinner given the year we came out. Long meals have completely gone out of fashion. Five courses are quite sufficient, but if they were presented with some variety, the hostesses would be astonished at the hearty appetites.

Don't ever think that you can give a successful coming-out

dinner without champagne. But inasmuch as none of the big restaurants serve liquor, it has to be sent ahead by the host. If you really want to, you may serve cocktails, but it is neither usual nor necessary. Actually you won't have to provide so much champagne, as the girls drink very little, if any, and the boys don't seem to drink much with their meals. They either arrive tight or get that way at the dance later in the evening. It's just the idea of the thing that counts.

The three days before the party are spent with no sleep, hanging on the telephone and sending wires to the young men who can't make up their minds about accepting or refusing. When at last the hostess knows how many people are coming to dinner, she can finish off the job by turning gray trying to seat them.

When the dinner is very large, it simplifies matters to seat the guests at several small tables. By small, we mean tables of ten or twelve. The parents are segregated with their particular intimates, while the rest of the tables are given over to the friends of the daughter. The seating is one part of the dinner the debutante herself should attend to if she can be persuaded to take enough interest. A mother can scarcely be expected to know that Amy Horne is never separated from Clarence Sott, or that Peggy Patt and Rupert Rippert haven't spoken since he put a snake in her dress at dancing school. At her own table she places her best friends, but she must think twice before selecting the young men to put on her right and left. These are honors reserved only for the most important guests, very good friends, or extremely serious beaux. The guests at the other tables are seated according to congeniality, not importance.

All the flowers sent to the heroine of the evening are made into a screen and used as a background for the mother, the father, and the deb (in that order) when they are receiving the guests. The bouquet carried by the debutante is the one provided by the family or her best beau. Some mothers and daughters feel that this is the occasion to use those long white gloves that have been reposing in the cupboard since Grandma was presented at court, but it really isn't necessary. After the guests have shaken hands with the host and made their pretty speeches, they are free to wander about. The men can hunt busily for the ladies who correspond to the names on the dinner cards they picked up in the ante-room. When at last dinner is announced (ordinarily at half past nine when it was scheduled for eight) the grown-ups file in first; then comes the debutante clinging to the favored youth who is to sit on her right, and the rest of the guests go in as best they can. This is one of the few occasions when a man is supposed to offer his arm to a lady. In the South, where, we are told, chivalry still persists, a lady takes a man's arm on every occasion. But in the North if a man gives you his arm, it is usually because he himself needs support. When a man and his dinner partner fail to connect, all they can do is wend their separate ways to the table and introduce themselves when they are finally seated.

Now begin a girl's difficulties for the evening.

She is probably sitting between two men whom she doesn't know, and must think of some way of opening the conversation, since they will almost invariably sit like bumps waiting for her to take the initiative. The most successful opening is a personal one. She has seen his name on the place card and, recognizing it, can say: "Aren't you a great friend of Laura Hart's?" Then they are off, discussing all of Laura's qualities and defects. Or, if he is obviously just down from college, she can ask him where he is getting an education and thus find friends in common. She needn't make an effort to appear brilliant—brains are a handicap to a debutante. All she has to do is to look vastly interested and amused at everything her neighbor says and keep up a steady flow of adjectives when he pauses for breath. Erudites do exist who insist upon going into a discussion of Hindu philosophy or Greek sculpture, and every now and then one of them will run across a little man with a pince-nez who after dinner will go around exclaiming: "What an interesting girl that Mabel Learned is!" But at the dance he will spend most of the evening cutting in on a belle who, if she has ever heard of Phidias, has the sense to keep it dark.

When there is a large ball, it is customary for the hostess of the dinner preceding to ask permission to take all her guests. If she doesn't, the wise young thing makes a date with some man to go on to the dance with him. If she has neglected to do this, it is up to her dinner partner to see that she gets there. Of course, he may not be invited to the ball; then she is in a real predicament. She can't ask him to crash the party, but neither can she arrive alone, because she will have no partner to start off with and, therefore, can never get on the dance floor. There are several ways out, however: she may appeal to the dinner hostess to provide an escort (this as the very last resort), or she may have a great friend at the ball whom she can ask to get her started, or, if she knows the hostess of the dance well, she can send her word to press an usher into action.

Lunches and Teas; Or, Scarcely Worth the Trouble

———— ◆ ————

Another, if somewhat inferior way of making a debut is a luncheon party. We have never been quite able to see the point of these entertainments, as only girls are invited (anywhere from fifty to three hundred) and we were always led to believe that a girl comes out to meet eligible men. These affairs usually take place at a restaurant or some female club, and the invitations are similar to those used for a dinner. The debutante and her mother, or whoever happens to be giving the luncheon, wear ordinary day clothes and hats and receive the guests in the doorway or any other convenient place. Since the guests can hardly go in two by two, each one is presented with a card when she checks her coat, indicating the number or the color of the table (too bad if you're color-blind).

For some unknown reason a corsage is placed at each cover. Usually it is made up of sweet peas or pinky-yellow roses, which, with their natural limpness and the heat of the room, look like bunches of weeds by the time they are pinned on. Even one camellia or gardenia would be preferable to any colored corsage.

It seems to be the rule for the guests to arrive late, and after the first course girls begin jumping up and saying good-by to their hostess, as they all seem to have something to do at two o'clock or shortly after. Consequently, half the meal is never eaten. There is no reason why a girl should go to a coming-out luncheon if she doesn't want to. Although there is invariably a group of debutantes who make a practice of going to every luncheon and actually seem to enjoy them, the majority admit that they are unbelievably dull. What could be a greater bore than getting all dressed up to go to an overheated restaurant filled with girls, most of whom one doesn't know, to eat bad food, poorly served, and end up with a limp bunch of flowers as the only reward?

The very conservative lean towards coming-out teas. It

is such a nice old-fashioned way of presenting a daughter to society—dignified, if not terribly amusing. A private house is the standard locale, but, failing this, a woman's club is highly suitable. As these functions are Old World anyway, they are the only ones at which a debutante sometimes asks one or several of her best friends to receive with her; just as at a dinner she carries a bouquet and stands surrounded by the flowers sent to her. The majority of debutantes choose this moment to go romantic and appear in an evening gown cut on *robe de style* lines, when a simple afternoon dress worn without a hat would be in far better taste and more chic. When there is dancing, as there usually is, the season's bud may join in after the first hour or so, when most of the guests have arrived. But even in the safety of her partner's arms she must keep a watchful eye on the floor and be ready to float gracefully over and greet one of the elderly ladies who have come to see "dear Hannah's little girl in her hour of triumph."

The guests are made up almost entirely of older ladies who dote on teas, but there are also the current debutantes, all the young men available, and friends of the family. It is no simple task to assemble a large number of young men for such an occasion, as none of this generation has had much tea discipline. Besides, it complicates their day, as they must rush home from their offices and change their clothes, arriving at the tea around six-thirty, just as everybody is ready to start home. In this case, changing their clothes seldom means anything more than washing up and putting on a dark suit, as only the old beaux seem to bother to get themselves into striped trousers and a cutaway.

In a private house the tea is served in the dining-room, and at a club in the room adjoining the ballroom. There is the usual array of cakes and sandwiches, with tea at one end of the table, and chocolate or coffee at the other. The servants take care of the guests, for asking a friend to "pour" has completely gone out. Pitchers of orangeade or lemonade are provided for the thirsty, and some reckless souls go so far as to serve champagne or a cup.

A coming-out tea is very pleasant if a debutante is to have a dinner or a dance also given in her honor. Both a luncheon and a tea are recognized as legitimate ways of coming out, but they don't make much effect. They're boring, and nobody is grateful for being bored or feels indebted to a hostess who has given a dull party. If they are given on account of economy, they fall short of their objective, for a luncheon costs as much as a small dinner, and what is spent on the corsages would pay for the champagne. Certainly teas and feminine lunches are not the most successful ways of launching a belle.

Coming Out to Music

———— ◆ ————

Every year fewer debutante balls are given in private homes. This is mainly due to the fact that people don't live in large houses any more. Besides, it is so much simpler to turn the whole thing over to experts in a hotel or restaurant, rather than have the inevitable disorder in one's own house.

There are ballrooms of every size in New York, so that it is no hard task to find one to accommodate a hundred or a thousand guests. The one great mistake is to engage a place too large, for somehow we moderns feel that a party is fun only in a crowded room, and an empty one spells a flop. But it is equally unsuccessful to try to put a throng that would overflow the Yale Bowl into the Ritz ballroom. The most ardent crowd-enthusiasts will admit that it is carrying things a bit too far to have such a crush that it is impossible to move around the floor, much less dance; where if one man cuts in on another, the first can't move away and the three remain together; and where any trailing pieces on the girl's dress are torn off.

Strangely enough, the hostess who depends upon ostentation for success and throws parties for a thousand people, with two orchestras which give the appearance of the Philharmonic out for the evening, artificial moonlight, and walls hung with cloth of silver and orchids, is more often criticized than praised by the guests, who never seem to enjoy these splurges as much as they do the simpler entertainments. When the rumor gets around that a ball is going to cost seventy-five or a hundred thousand dollars, the guests go to drink up the liquor, and assume the same attitude they would if they were going to see one of the season's musical super-extravaganzas.

Invitations to any dance or ball should be sent out at least a month beforehand or, for a popular date, six weeks, but never sooner. They are similar to those for a large dinner except that "your" may quite correctly be engraved in place of the guest's name. In the case of a sudden death in the family the invitations must be recalled. An announcement may be inserted in two or three of the leading newspapers, or else an engraved card sent to every person who has accepted.

It is absolutely impossible to give a successful party, much less a successful ball, without serving liquor. It has never yet been done and probably never will be. And, what's more, it certainly doesn't guarantee a sober evening, for if it is known that it is to be a dry party, the young men will bring flasks or fortify themselves before arriving. If they don't discover the lack of liquid stimulant until after their arrival, they will hasten into the nearest speakeasy between dances. The ball probably ends early, for half the stags have had the sense to go home before they had to be carried, and most of the others have curled up happily in any convenient place. Champagne should flow at supper-time, although there needn't be any beforehand or afterwards. It is a grand but expensive gesture to serve champagne throughout the evening.

Although the receiving line has gone completely out of fashion, at a big ball the debutante still asks her best men friends to act as ushers. Each one is given a red and white carnation to wear in his buttonhole, which is supposed to distinguish him from the other guests. His duties consist in seeing that everybody has a good time, looking after stray foreigners and strangers from other cities, and finding a man to cut in on couples who appear to be hopelessly stuck. He may introduce a man whom he has never seen before to a girl who is also a stranger to him. Therefore, any youth who feels that he cannot live without meeting the girl in the pink tulle may take his troubles to the nearest usher.

Aside from the honor, the only thing an usher gets out of it all is the right to dance with any girl in the room without being introduced.

Otherwise, there is more glory than pleasure attached to this distinction; that is, if it's taken seriously, which seldom happens. To give the young men their due, it must be said that they are more or less reliable until midnight. Then they have a strange way of disappearing; so if you feel that you're going to need the services of an usher, you'd better arrive on time.

The hosts, including the debutante, should contribute something towards the enjoyment of the guests. At a small party it is fairly easy to see that people are introduced to each other, but at a large ball all they can do is keep their eyes open for girls who appear to be stuck and prod the ushers into action. In any event, plenty of liquor, a long stag line, a good orchestra, and lots of pretty girls are what go to make a successful party.

Ten-thirty or eleven is the usual hour for a dance to begin. The hosts must be on hand at the entrance of the ballroom at that hour, and the debutante should remain at her post until midnight, looking radiant and greeting all the arrivals with equal cordiality.

Supper at a ball is always "sit down," never buffet, and at about one o'clock it is announced by strains of martial music. Not every girl in the room hears this sound with the same emotions. If you have a supper partner, it is all great fun and you look forward to the rest and food with pleasure; but if you haven't made a date until that moment, there is no worse sound in the world. If the man you are dancing with at the time the music is played is free, you may be saved, for he will probably ask you to have supper with him. Unfortunately, few young men have the tact to come right out and either say: "Will you have supper with me?" or, if they are engaged: "Can I find your partner for you?" They invariably ask: "Have you a supper partner?" which puts a poor girl in a quandary, as she doesn't know whether he is giving an invitation or making an effort to get rid of her. He may offer to find someone for her, but if she is too proud to admit that she hasn't been dated up, she can only ask him to take her to the foot of the stairs, where she is to meet a mythical partner. When she does this, she has no choice but to go home, as she can never return to the ballroom unattended. If you have a supper partner, but have agreed to be at the same table with several friends, you may always tell an extra man to come along. But you must sit beside the man who first asked you.

The hostess has her own table in the supper room, at which she seats her best friends and the ushers. It's just as well to tell them of this beforehand, so that they will make no other arrangements.

Cutting In and Sitting Out

———— ◆ ————

Cutting in has become a regular Frankenstein monster, for it has gone beyond our control. It is the cause of so many odd men being invited to parties, since at a successful dance there must be at least three men to every girl. The result is that almost any trousered thing is called in to make up the stag line. It is possible to meet anybody, from a barber to a dentist or a veterinary, at one of the enormous so-called "smart" coming-out balls.

The stag line has ceased to be a line and has become a large block in the middle of the room—a regiment of young men who take up most of the floor and make dancing almost impossible. The effort required to dance with attractive girls only is usually too much for a stag, as he can't go two steps without being cut in on, and then comes the exertion of darting into the crowd again in search of a partner. On the other hand, nobody wants to get stuck, so that finally the struggle of dancing with belles becomes so great that he goes out and quietly gets tight. No stag will take a chance on getting stuck with any girl and having to spend the evening with her. Duty dancing is an unknown phrase to most youths. They may have been to a girl's house two or three times, but if they think they are going to get hooked for long, they won't dance with her. There was even one occasion when a hostess remained stuck for three hours at her own party. Of course, nobody may have been aware that she *was* the hostess.

The majority of men, when questioned, will admit that they don't like the cutting-in system, yet it is kept on year after year. But the girls who are belles love it because they think that being "broken" every five seconds displays their popularity to the whole room. They fail to realize that being surrounded by a large group of men, all clamoring at once for dances, exhibits success far more effectively. It is true, however, that the system of engaging dances ahead, as practiced in England, can be deadly. One dance goes on forever, and even if a party doesn't break up until six in the morning, there have seldom been more than twelve numbers. In Montreal the procedure seems to be a very practical one. For instance, there a man asks a girl for the third dance, and cutting in is permitted when the encore is played, but not before. In this way the men get around to all the girls, and if one gets stuck with his partner during the encore, he can leave her at the beginning of the next number. And the girl who has no partner can disappear into the dressing-room and keep in hiding until the next dance on her card; nobody need know where she is, and she is saved the humiliation of being stuck.

Getting stuck doesn't seem serious to a person who has been out for several years, but it is a very real tragedy to a girl of eighteen. To begin with, her partner will never do a thing to help her out and looks gloomier and gloomier by the moment. They stumble wearily and silently around the floor, and we have heard that a man sometimes even goes to the extent of waving a dollar bill behind the girl's back in order to induce a stag to cut in. There was a debutante to whom this actually happened. She caught her partner in the act and was sufficiently quick-witted to say: "Make it five and I'll go home." The story got around and she was the belle of the ball.

If all debutantes could acquire that much indifference and aplomb, they would have a better time than they do by worrying, for that is one of the reasons why girls usually enjoy their second and third seasons more than they do their first; by that time, getting stuck doesn't hold the same terrors for them. A heavy beau who will look after her can be of tremendous assistance to a debutante, as he gives her a feeling of assurance. It can all be such a nightmare. Even the girl who ordinarily has a good time can never tell when she will have the bad luck to go to a party where there won't be many of her particular friends.

The deb who wants to be popular must have the endurance of a Spartan and the training of a Southerner. No matter how tired she is, how ill she may feel, or how bored, she must seem to be enjoying herself immensely and give the impression of having a pogo stick concealed beneath her skirts. The one who feels sure that she is stuck after the first few steps and gets a set, wooden expression on her face might as well go home then, for she is finished. But if she looks vastly amused and laughs hilariously, some man is bound to cut in, just out of curiosity, to find out what is so funny. Debutante, keep smiling! It's your only hope.

There are a few rules for cutting in: Tom is dancing with

Mary when Dick breaks. Tom cannot cut right back in. He must wait until another man is dancing with Mary. If Mary is sitting out with Harry, nobody may interrupt. A stag must wait until she is back on the floor again before cutting in.

A girl doesn't ask a man to sit out; the suggestion must always come from him. Of course, she can get round this by saying she is thirsty. When a drink has been obtained, it is only natural to sit out while sipping it. Some men say they like having their partner make the first move towards a sofa, for if they ask her to sit out, she can hardly refuse and they can never know whether it is really what she wants to do. These modest creatures are the exception, however, and it is usually safer to let the man suggest sitting out.

Sitting out in cars at parties in the country isn't such a good idea. There are usually but two reasons why a man asks a girl to go out to a car with him; one is that he wants a swig out of his flask. A girl who accepts an invitation of that sort usually knows what is expected; if she doesn't, she will find out soon enough. Hostesses at country places should provide sufficient sitting-out space so that the guests will not have to take to cars unless they deliberately wish to do so.

That Certain
Something

—— ◆ ——

L earn to dance before you come out. Being a good dancer may not make you a belle, but treading on the stags' toes will certainly prevent you from becoming one. If you have a suspicion that you're a bit heavy, or notice that you can't seem to keep away from your partner's knees, don't be proud; take a few dancing lessons. Do think of your appearance. Hold yourself straight and try to avoid that strange twisted posture so prevalent among the very young. Only a debutante can understand why putting her head on her partner's shoulder and playing London Bridge with the rest of her anatomy should bear any resemblance to dancing. It may be partly due to the collegiate grip—the man pulling his right arm under the girl's left armpit and winding it around her neck. If you get one of these contortionists, don't be timid about asking him to put his arm lower. He may leer at you, but at least you won't get a crick in your neck.

There never was a sub-debutante who didn't imagine herself in the role of a great belle the year she came out. Even the ugliest duckling hopes for a miraculous transformation, or feels sure that if only people get a chance to know her, they will find that she has a subtle charm and a certain glamour. If one could only prescribe the elements that go towards the making of a belle, everything would be much simpler. Unfortunately, the greatest attributes, personality and sex appeal, are indefinable, and you have to be born with them. But the all-important "line" is something which can be cultivated. The words and phrases don't matter—some people can do it with a look. The object is to give the young man you're after the feeling that he is the most wonderful creature on earth. Of course, good looks, assurance, and vivacity count for a great deal, but they won't put you across if you lack that certain something; if you've got it, you don't need any other qualifications.

The Great Step

———— ◆ ————

When we think of how engagements and weddings used to be celebrated, our own fashion seems a bit casual. The announcement of an engagement was the signal for the whole countryside to pay a formal call to drink to the health and happiness of the affianced pair. A year or two then elapsed. To get married sooner than nine months after the betrothal was considered unseemly haste. The wedding day approached, and ornate silver, heavy cut glass, statues of little Negroes hopefully extending card-salvers, began to pour in from all sides. Distant cousins, aunts, and uncles the bride had never seen, rolled into town in carriages, and relatives crowded the house to the very attic. There were festivities for a week, and the eating, drinking, and dancing continued until the day of the ceremony. Then all the guests thronged decorously into the church to watch the bride float slowly up the aisle under a cloud of tulle and lace that hid the blushes which rose at the memory of Mamma's embarrassed exposition of the facts of life.

Now an engagement may be announced by the parents of the bride-to-be at a dinner at which the guests are told the news as they arrive, or Papa proposes a toast to the happy pair at the salad or dessert course. This last, however, is an outmoded procedure. The more modern content themselves with publishing the news in the papers. The necessary details are given either by telephone or by letter to several of the conservative newspapers. Even if you have a prejudice against having your personal affairs made a part of the daily news, it is better policy to send in a full account. Give particulars concerning both families, and where the young people were educated. If the engaged pair are of any prominence, a reporter will probably be sent up to get an interview.

They must never fail to write notes to their respective relatives and intimate friends, timing the letters to arrive a day or two before the news is made public. Only a few lines or a telegram will be expected, but no one entitled to such a letter should be overlooked as he will take it as a slight. Friends who live at some distance should write their best wishes and congratulations; the others may telephone. Incidentally, the girl receives best wishes, and the man congratulations.

According to strict rules of etiquette, the man's parents must call on his future wife within twenty-four hours of the announcement. Actually, this is the exception rather than the rule. There doesn't seem to be much point to it, for it would be strange for a girl never to have met her fiancé's parents until after the engagement, unless, of course, they live in another city. And if they do, it might be rather difficult for them to pay their formal call within the time prescribed by strict etiquette. She takes him to meet her relatives and friends, but his must come to her.

The romantic moment when the boy tenderly slips the ring on the girl's finger, brushing her cheek with a kiss, may take place at the time of the proposal or several days later, but the ring should not be worn publicly until after the announcement. The stone and setting greatly depend upon personal taste, although there seems to be a feeling that a solitaire diamond is the only possible choice. Actually, any stone will do, and if the pocketbook is limited, it seems to us that a really good guard ring would be preferable to a dinky diamond. The couple may exchange engagement presents, but it is not obligatory and hardly customary. Members of the family and very close friends often feel called upon to make some gift, and although it's nice for the engaged ones, there is no real necessity for it.

Friends are expected to give parties before the wedding, but showers have definitely gone out in fashionable circles. It does seem to be asking too much of bridesmaids and friends to contribute something to a shower as well as give an adequate wedding present. As a rule an engagement party takes the form of a dinner. Often the couple will be seated next to each other, which is absolutely incorrect! They are both guests of honor, and therefore the girl should be on the right of the host, and the man on the right of the hostess.

By the time a pair have reached the engagement stage there doesn't seem to be much need for chaperonage. After all, he has shown his willingness to do right by Nell, so a mother can forget her worries. At this point she should let her daughter decide whether she is going to the altar in bridal white with a clear conscience.

All eyes are upon an engaged couple, for everybody is interested in them; so they should try to assume the right manner. This is no easy task, as they must register devotion without being so stickily sentimental that they bore and embarrass everybody around them. On the other hand, they shouldn't indulge in intimate quarrels in public, any more than should married couples.

When an engagement is broken, an announcement should be sent to the papers. No matter what the cause of the breach, it is inserted by the girl's parents and has but one form: "Mr. and Mrs. John Henry Beekman announce that the engagement of their daughter Helena, to Mr. Elihu Rufus Sutton, has been broken by mutual consent." The ring and other gifts of value must be returned to the ex-fiancé, as well as engagement presents received from relatives and friends. Then all they can do is sit back and endure the ensuing notoriety and publicity with the best grace they can muster. Although flight may not be the bravest, it is certainly the easiest course for the girl, in a situation like this. Retiring to a hospital won't help, but a trip to Europe will get you away from it all.

In a Cloud of Tulle

— ◆ —

An invitation to be a bridesmaid is an honor which cannot be declined without some very good reason. Our idea of one of the better reasons is the impending arrival of a little stranger. The bride feels that she must ask an old friend to be in her wedding, but any lady in this interesting condition should have the grace to refuse. We know that symbols of fertility are appropriate to the marriage ceremony, but they needn't be quite so obviously borne in on the congregation, not to mention the timorous groom, whose nerves are usually shot anyhow. Only intimate friends or relatives are asked to be bridesmaids, and their number should never exceed twelve, unless the wedding is to look as though it had been staged by

Mr. Carroll. A sister or very close friend is the maid of honor. They all receive presents from the bride, but are supposed to pay for their own costumes. If the bride's taste runs to lamé or sable-bordered skirts, however, she should pay at least half the bill, particularly as such dresses are usually too bizarre and impractical to be worn again.

Our modern taste for simplicity and our feeling of impermanence are never more strongly shown than in the present-day trousseau. This used to contain enough household linen to stock a large hotel, and so much personal linen (literally linen) that the wife was still wearing a trousseau nightgown with a tatted yoke on her silver wedding anniversary. Now it consists of just enough linen for the bride's house (marked with her maiden initials, like the silver), a dozen sets of undies, more elaborate than she wore as a young girl, and a wardrobe for one season.

The wedding dress itself may be of silk, satin, brocade, lace, velvet, organdie, or chiffon, but it must be white. Of late there has been a vogue for cloth of gold, pale pink, green, yellow, or other pastel shades. A singular choice indeed, considering that pure white is symbolic! Are the girls who wear colors ignorant of this, or are they too honest to face the world in spotless white?

The bride's parents bear practically the whole expense of a wedding. It is they who pay for the trousseau, presents to the bridesmaids, their bouquets, the father's boutonnière, the decorations in the church, the music (choir, organist, and soloist), the fee to the sexton, photographs, boxes of wedding cake, motors for the bridal party, and the one in which the bride and groom drive away. The groom pays for the wedding ring, the marriage license, the bride's bouquet, the bachelor dinner, gifts to the best man and the ushers, their ties, gloves, and boutonnières, his own boutonnière, the clergyman's fee, and the honeymoon.

Again we must refer you to a jeweler for the details of wording and engraving wedding invitations. They are always sent out by the bride's family, although the groom makes out a list of his friends whom he wishes to invite. If the bride's parents are divorced, the invitation is usually issued in the mother's name, unless the girl has been in the entire custody of her father. If she's an orphan, her nearest relative does the inviting. Failing one, she has no choice but to invite the guests in her own name. Engraved announcements, timed so that they will arrive on the evening of the wedding or the next day, are mailed to acquaintances who don't receive invitations.

It used to be the custom for the bachelor dinner to take place the night before the wedding. Now, however, the bridesmaids' and ushers' dinner is usually on that night, for a groom realizes that he and his attendants need some time in which to recover sufficiently to be able to distinguish the altar from the organ and walk up the aisle with no mishaps. These bachelor dinners are made up of the groom, the best man, and the ushers; a stag party in fact. This is not the occasion to invite the entire chorus of a musical comedy to add to the gayety.

The rehearsal takes place the day before the wedding. All the attendants practice their parts, but the bride looks on. Her place is taken by one of the other girls, for it is considered bad luck for the bride and groom to stand at the altar or walk down the aisle together before the actual ceremony.

The presents should begin arriving as soon as the invitations are issued. Even friends of the groom who have never met the bride send their offerings directly to her. The only possible way to keep track of the gifts and the donors is to enter them in a book kept for that purpose. If this is done as soon as they are unwrapped, there will be no danger of thanking Mrs. Vanderrich for a lace antimacassar when she sent a golden cornucopia. There is no way of getting out of writing a thank-you note for each present. When possible, it should be done before the wedding, but in any case it is in appallingly bad taste to send out cards like one that was brought to our notice, which read: "Your present has been received and will be acknowledged in due course."

The bride who receives so many gifts that she cannot possibly acknowledge them all should engage a secretary to write personal notes to the people who don't know her handwriting. The perfect time for displaying presents is at the reception, but when it takes place in a house too small to spare a separate room, friends are invited in a few days before to see them. The bride's and groom's gifts to each other are invariably something for personal use.

Now, at last, all arrangements have been made for the wedding. The day finally arrives and the bride and groom are so weary from preparations and parties that the whole thing is likely to take on the unreality of a dream. The ceremony probably takes place at the fashionable hour of four, although some people prefer noon. In the South evening weddings are popular, but in the East they are not at all smart. The bride drives to the church with her father in a car provided by him. In a large city she may have a police escort, which, although seldom indispensable, adds importance and a thrill to the occasion. Her motor is the last to arrive and waits in front of the church until she comes out to drive away with her husband in the place of her father. It is, alas, no longer customary to decorate the bridal motor with ribbons, orange blossoms, and other bouquets of white flowers. The only concession made to the occasion is that the tires are painted white, and the chauffeur wears a white boutonnière and white gloves.

When the bride's father is dead, she is given away by her brother or nearest male relative, or, failing any of these, her godfather or guardian. There is no set rule against it, but it is unusual for a mother to perform this duty.

Today, when there is likely to be one divorce in every family, the question of who is to give the bride away, or where the various sets of parents are to sit, is one fraught with complications. A father who has retained partial custody of his daughter leads her to the altar, and the presence or absence of the mother's second husband is decided by the individuals. A girl who was very young when her mother remarried, and who has been completely estranged from her real father is given away by her stepfather, and the former doesn't appear at all.

Lately there was actually a marriage at which both the

bride's and the groom's parents were divorced and remarried, and none of them were on speaking terms. Matters were further complicated by the fact that, according to all the rules of seating, the bride's family had to be together in the pews on the left of the altar, and the groom's on the right. It was all finally settled by each one's arriving without the current husband or wife, and sitting in separate pews, although on the same side of the church.

Inasmuch as the reception can under no circumstances take place in the groom's home, the bride with a small house or apartment has no choice but to engage the ballroom of a hotel or club. If a relative or friend offers her a place, so much the better, but the bride's family are still expected to pay all the expenses.

The whole wedding party has to find some convenient place in which to spread out to receive the guests—first the mother of the bride, then the groom's mother and father, the groom, the bride, the maid of honor, and finally the brides-maids. The bride's father seems to have no duty but to wander around and look after guests. The ushers are supposed to lead up old friends and distinguished guests—a duty they attend to with alacrity, as each person gives them another chance to kiss the bridesmaids.

Some kind of music should be provided, if only to fill in gaps between exclamations of "Doesn't Helena look lovely? What a handsome couple!" If there is dancing, the guests can't take to the floor until the "happy pair" have made one turn around the room.

When there aren't any bridesmaids, the bride invites her most intimate girl friends to sit at her table to keep the ushers amused. With a full bridal party the bride is on the right of the groom, with the best man on her right, and the maid of honor on the groom's left. Whatever happens, there should be plenty of champagne in which to drink the couple's health and to liven up the spirits of the guests who, unless they are confirmed wedding-goers, will by then be bored to extinction.

Girls who are marrying divorced men or widowers and realize that it's in better taste to have a simple ceremony, or who for some other reason want a small wedding, often decide to have an altar set up in the drawing-room and be married at home. To us a house wedding falls into the same class with an amateur theatrical performance given in a garden. We feel that as long as you are going in for this archaic ritual, you might as well do it in a big way or get married in a registry office or church vestry. A house wedding lacks beauty, dignity, and solemnity. But who could feel solemn standing before an improvised altar, surrounded by caterers' gilt chairs, with the kitchen-maid peering through the lilies?

There is seldom time to engrave cards announcing a broken-off wedding, so they may be printed and sent to all the friends who have received invitations. The papers are also notified, with the time-worn phrase: "Mr. and Mrs. John Henry Beekman announce that the marriage which had been arranged between their daughter Helena and Mr. Elihu Rufus Sutton will not take place." This is another occasion when presents must be returned and a trip to Europe is in order. In the case of a sudden death in the family a wedding is seldom postponed, but all the invitations, except those for members of the two families, are recalled.

Twice Shy — ?

— ◆ —

According to all custom, a widow is supposed to wait a year before remarrying. But nowadays, when, with the exception of sticklers for outworn conventions, no one goes into mourning for longer than two months, if at all, and when widows' weeds have practically disappeared, a man's relict remarries when the notion strikes her.

For a second marriage a lady has to content herself with a quiet ceremony in a chapel or at home, if she doesn't want to be married by a magistrate. Having, it is to be hoped, lost her right to white satin she wears a simple afternoon frock and hat. Any attempt at the unusual, such as a Russian costume with a colored veil flowing from the head-dress, is not only dowdy but ridiculous, as are all similar attempts at originality. She has discarded her first engagement and wedding ring before announcing her second engagement.

In this practical matter-of-fact day, elopements have lost all their romance. To begin with, parents don't seem to have much fight left, and, whatever happens, there is never the necessity of slipping down a ladder in the dead of night into the arms of an impetuous lover. The whole idea of an elopement is a bit silly and immature. If you are really determined to marry a man whom your family doesn't like, you can nearly always talk them into letting you have your own way.

We won't attempt to give an example of the correct wording for the note which is left on the pincushion, especially as it's doubtful if the parents would notice whether or not the form were correct. The more up-to-date way of breaking the news to the family is to send a wire after all is over and it is too late to interfere. When they become reconciled to the marriage, they send out announcements just as they would under ordinary circumstances.

This book is primarily intended for girls and young women and would, therefore, on first thought not include special information for divorcees. Since Reno has shortened its time of residence, however, it is not uncommon for a girl of twenty-one to be once divorced and starting out with a second husband. Things move so fast that you scarcely realize that your friends are even thinking of separating until you see a laconic announcement in the paper or one of the magazines devoted to the activities of the fashionable.

A divorcee keeps her engagement ring as well as any other jewels given to her by her former husband. But she seldom continues to wear the wedding band—not that she probably wore it much when she was married. She is no longer Mrs. Elihu Rufus Sutton; she has become Mrs. Beekman Sutton. Just as friends are supposed to be told of an engagement before the news is made public, they should receive notes warning them of the impending divorce. It will save much embarrassment.

Divorce has become so simple, and scandal is so seldom attached to it, that ex-husbands and wives feel no animosity towards each other, and friends are not expected to take sides. It's all done in such a friendly spirit that it is not unusual for a man to go to the station to meet his former wife when she returns proudly bearing her decree. Things have gone so far that the case is known of a lady who sent her fiancé to meet her husband when he came to town for the divorce hearing.

That evening this modern triangle, with the two friendly perjurers who had acted as witnesses, all went out on a bender to celebrate the engagement. A little confusing, perhaps, but oh, so pleasant and amicable!

Travel Broadens
the Mind

———— ◆ ————

Travel is the one pursuit which never loses its lure, probably because it offers so much variety. No matter how many years you spend in going from one place to another, there always remains some new country to see, some strange land to explore. You can be so fed up with boats, trains, and motor cars that you feel like a little girl we knew who, after journeying eighteen thousand miles, put down her small suitcase with a bang and announced: "When I travel to where I'm traveling to, I'm never going to travel any more." Yet a month later this same little girl was packing up her dolls, frantic with joy at the thought of getting on the train again.

There is a science to travel which is perfected only with

time and experience. It's when you reach the point of going through the routine automatically that you become a successful traveler, and even then you can't get along without a calm temperament and a sense of humor. Getting all wrought up seldom helps except, of course, in Latin countries, where the moment invariably arrives when you have to outshout porters, cab-drivers, and even customs officials. But take our advice and don't try the same tactics over here or in England. Coolness, efficiency, and a knack for taking difficulties for granted and losing no time in overcoming them will do as much towards getting you round the world as a well-lined purse.

Buying tickets, checking trunks, and all the other details of travel should form a part of every person's education. It is true that the clinging vine has tremendous appeal, but even the most protective of males will soon weary of the helpless little flower who is proud of the fact that she is incapable of buying her own ticket or getting herself, with all her luggage, from New York to Philadelphia.

It has been some time since it was considered improper for an unmarried, not to say young, girl to travel without some form of chaperonage. In these progressive times one is only mildly astonished to hear of an eighteen-months-old infant being transported by plane from New York to Chicago, with no more protection than a luggage tag around its neck. Of course, the perils that beset the path of the beauteous maiden are slightly different from those encountered by a baby; but we fear that any young girl who gets into difficulties on a crowded train or ship must be out looking for them with bright and avid eyes. A pretty girl traveling alone will always arouse interest, but so long as she is quiet and well behaved, she can go from one end of the country to the other and stay alone in hotels without fear of being molested.

The only way to avoid being picked up is to develop the psychology of the averted eye. Never appear to see the people about you, and don't look directly at anybody. There are three ancient and tried ways of scraping up an acquaintance—offering a magazine, volunteering to open or close a window, and helping to lift a heavy suitcase. You have no choice but to accept these services with politeness, but you needn't put any inviting warmth into your thanks. There is a manner which is a mixture of civility and indifference that should put off the most insistent picker-upper, although every now and then one has the bad luck to encounter a pushing, thick-skinned individual who can only catch the point when you are out-and-out rude. On short trips a person who deliberately tries to pick you up deserves a rebuff. But on journeys lasting for several days one becomes more tolerant, as conversing, even with a stranger, relieves the terrible monotony. In the dining-car you sit at the table with people whom you've never seen before. You are not expected to talk to them, but it is only courteous to acknowledge their presence with a slight smile on sitting down and on leaving the table.

On the train you are fairly safe, for you have the protection of all the other passengers, as well as the porter. That is why it is better for a young girl traveling alone to take a berth rather than a compartment. But no matter how charming a train acquaintance may seem, it is always risky to accept a lift in a car from the station to your hotel.

It appears that it is most improper for a lady to invite a male acquaintance whom she happens to meet on the train to sit with her in her section or compartment or to eat her meals with him. This is just absurd. If you happen to have known a man all your life, you can scarcely cut him dead just because you are afraid that a trainful of strangers will think you are traveling together. By all means see him as often as you like if it amuses you. You should attempt to pay for your own meals, although if your companion insists upon paying the check, there is no good reason why you shouldn't let him. But you must never allow a man whom you have just met to spend a penny on you.

On long journeys a woman pays her own expenses and buys her own ticket (not merely because of the Mann Act). On a short trip, to a house party, for example, it is carrying punctiliousness to an extreme not to allow your escort to attend to everything. If you know he is hard up, you can use feminine tact and get your ticket ahead of time, agreeing to meet him on the train.

.

Never Speak to Strangers Unless They Speak to You

———— ◆ ————

The main object, when traveling, is to remain inconspicuous at all times. That's why one's costume should be chosen with care and with as much attention to correctness as one would devote to riding clothes. As in these, simplicity and practicality are the most important features. A smart suit of some dark material, or a very plain dress under a coat, with a small brimmed hat (the object being to hide as much hair as possible and keep it in place) is the obvious choice. One of the most important accessories is a leather pocketbook large enough to contain money, tickets, passport, several handkerchiefs, and all the other odds and ends that somehow seem to find their way into the traveler's purse. You must look neat;

therefore never pin on corsages, as they are not only incorrect with day clothes, but look too dismal when they start to droop after half an hour on a heated train. Velvet, satin, crepe georgette, or chiffon dresses, large, drooping hats, or tiny dressy ones with fancy veils, white kid gloves, patent leather or satin pumps, buckled shoes, and dazzling jewelry, are all indications of the inexperienced traveler, not to say the person of vulgar taste.

Just as in a hotel, when a waiter brings in your breakfast tray, you don't bother about grabbing for your clothes, on a train you may feel free to go from your berth to the dressing-room in your kimono and mules.

More or less the same clothes are worn for traveling on the water as on land, except that on shipboard tweeds and business-like sports costumes are more practical. A pair of low-heeled shoes should always be included in the luggage, as it is difficult, not to say dangerous to walk the decks on high heels if the ship is rolling or pitching. You always dress for dinner, but carry the same simplicity that marks your day-time clothes into the ones you wear for evening. Very décolleté creations of tulle or spangles look ridiculous and make one wonder whether the people who wear them haven't any other place in which to show them off. Consider a ship as you would a hotel and don't appear in the public rooms in pyjamas or a negligee.

As soon as you get on the ship, go to the chief steward and reserve your dining-room table. Our advice to anyone traveling alone would be to take a table for one, for you never know whom you are going to draw for a dining-room companion, and once you have made an acquaintance on shipboard, it is practically impossible to get rid of him. After you've had time to look the field over, you can go about finding companions to keep you from being too bored.

Sitting at the captain's table is an honor reserved for distinguished passengers. Although it limits your freedom, inasmuch as you are expected, to put in an appearance and to arrive more or less on time for meals, it is pleasant for the lone traveler, for he has company and is somewhat protected from the advances of other passengers, by appearing to be in a group. Anxious mothers whose young sons and daughters are traveling alone may write to the captain asking him to keep an eye on them, in which case he usually puts them at his table.

Each guest is assigned to a place at table according to precedence, so don't flop into the first chair you see. You buy your own wine, and it is customary to go into the lounge after dinner and have coffee with your table companions. If the captain asks you to join him for a cocktail, coffee, or a game of some sort, you have to accept and like it. He will often not be present at the table; in fact, he never puts in an appearance on the first and last evenings or in bad weather. If you don't see him to say good-by, write him a bread-and-butter note. Ask the dining-room steward how to write the superscription, as titles vary. Take all your other troubles to the purser and don't forget that you are supposed to greet a ship's officer whenever you see him.

A girl who happens to be traveling on the same ship with a man she knows need not hesitate to share a table with him or have his deck chair placed next to hers. The other passengers will probably die of curiosity wondering what their relationship is and will be certain they are traveling in sin, but we wouldn't worry about that.

Garrulous strangers may be a nuisance on the train, but they are nothing compared to what one finds on a ship. There seems to be something about the sea air that loosens tongues and inspires people with a craving to make friends. As the rules which govern speaking to strangers on land don't hold at sea, it makes life difficult for anyone wishing privacy. It is taken for granted that your neighbor on deck will speak to you, but the man who deliberately walks up to you when you are going around the deck, or calmly sits down at your table in the smoking-room, comes under the heading of a pick-up. You should be chilly with him, for he will usually turn out to be a tactless bore. It is so easy to find an opportunity to speak to someone casually when you are sitting next to each other at the bar or are in the swimming-pool, or even the reading-room, that the other means of attack shows a certain lack of breeding. If someone asks you to join in a game of deck tennis or shuffleboard, accept if you feel like playing. The encounter carries no obligation and you need show only a slight sign of recognition afterwards.

A lady wanders in and out of the bar or smoking-room quite alone and unaccompanied, but in the evening don't sit alone in the ballroom unless you're in the mood to be picked up by every stray man in the place. If you are in a party, you will be more or less protected from eager dance-enthusiasts, and it will be quite easy to get rid of them with a curt refusal.

On no account permit a person whom you have just met to go with you to your cabin, even with the ostensible purpose of leaving a package or a book. And at night always lock your door, even if you've never done it before in your life. Even though you don't insist upon privacy, have a thought for your valuables.

Two nights before docking there is usually a benefit for a sailors' charity fund. There is no way in which you can get out of appearing and donating something, if only a small sum. Professionals and amateurs with any real talent have no choice but to agree to perform with good grace. In fact, if you are asked to assist in any way—speak, auction off gifts, or collect money—you can't refuse.

Traveling by motor is just one situation after another. You have to make up your mind to take the minimum amount of luggage, and if the car isn't your own, whatever you take will be too much. If you're on the front seat, you have to think twice before lighting a cigarette, because ashes and sparks will be blown onto the people behind you. You're never sure about the driver. He may be careless, absent-minded, short-sighted, and drunk—only intent on getting places as quickly as possible. All you can do is sit tight and hope that the glass is unbreakable. No matter what happens, don't scream; a scream at the wrong moment has often been known to cause a stall. Then, of course, there are always break-downs and the question of where to spend the night. So long as there are no overnight stops, it is all right to motor alone with a man.

Air travel presents fewer difficulties. At least your mind is at ease about the pilot, for you know that he's been physically examined within an inch of his life and that he's cold sober. There are regulations about smoking and you will soon discover that you can't take all your trunks and pets with you unless you are willing to pay more than the ticket cost you for excess baggage. Anybody who might want to pick you up would have to do it by letter, as the noise of the motors precludes any conversation. All you have to do is sit quietly, make all preparations for the worst (don't be optimistic just because you've never been seasick), and pray that you'll arrive right side up.

Out of Town

———— ◆ ————

At last we have acquired the European custom of relaxing when we go on a vacation. We don't bother about large important entertainments or dressy clothes. At summer resorts and tropical winter playgrounds life is extremely informal. Most invitations to big parties are by telegram, friends drop in on each other at all hours to go swimming, and luncheon is buffet whether eaten at home or in the beach clubhouse.

Social rules and distinctions are relaxed. Practically anybody who can give a good party is accepted. The result is that many people consider resorts as opening wedges into society. Usually they are wasting their time and money, for contacts made at these places are seldom taken seriously. Although it's a reflection on society, there is no doubt about it that, once back in town, these new acquaintances are completely ignored.

In most summer resorts bathing-suits, shorts, and pyjamas are worn all day long, and a frock is hardly ever seen except at tea-time or in the evening. There are only two types of clothes, sports and evening. Simplicity is the keynote—none of your dainty frills and baby laces. In the places where one always changes for dinner, it is considered better taste to wear simple evening frocks. Trailing ball gowns are left behind for town wear. Hats are worn only by those who wish to keep their hair in place or shade their eyes, and gloves are seldom pulled on except when driving a car. Only old ladies cling to their stockings, and not so many of them. Although some elderly dames keep their million-dollar pearls clasped around their throats even when they are going fishing, it is neither wise nor correct to wear any important jewelry with sports clothes. If you are sentimental about your engagement ring, it can be made the one exception.

The bathing-suit has become the real daytime resort uniform. From the first morning swim to the last dip just before cocktail-time the day is a succession of changes, but only from a wet suit to a dry one. It has become the ideal tennis costume unless you happen to prefer shorts. You lounge around, you lie in the sun in the briefest possible swimming-togs, you keep them on for lunch, only adding a pair of slacks or a short beach-coat. If cocktail-time still finds you near the water, you sit in a friend's cabaña in the same undressed state. Abroad we have seen tea dancers merely clad in bathing-suits causing no comment. But over here people are apt to be a little more shockable; so add some sort of leg-covering before taking to the dance floor. All towns situated near beaches have grown so hardened to the sight of semi-clad humanity that one can drive or go shopping in pyjamas or shorts without fear of the law or public opinion.

The one unforgivable sin is to try to look pretty-pretty. A good sunburn does away with the necessity of repairing make-up every few minutes, so if you keep lipstick on, the rest of your face will take care of itself. The girl who tries to keep up that beautifully groomed appearance stands out, but only because she looks out of place among all the other healthy people who have returned to nature. The idea is to be comfortable. The more comfortable you look, the more correct you are.

Summer,
Winter, Spring

———— ◆ ————

Newport is the only resort which has retained any of its earlier elegance and formality and in which an outsider hasn't a chance. Even there, the old guard has had to give in to the preferences of youth to the extent of permitting stockingless bathers in backless suits on Bailey's Beach. They qualify this, however, with a ruling that coats must be worn on the sands. But nobody pays any attention to it. The middle of the week is fairly quiet, just as in any other place, but over the week-end there are always dinners and at least one formal dance, not to say ball. The men arrive from town on Friday evening just in time to struggle with white ties, for this is the only summer resort in the world where full evening dress is de rigueur.

In the latter part of August the real season ends in a blaze of glory with Tennis Week. There is a dinner and a dance every night, but Friday and Saturday are the days chosen by the hosts giving the two most important balls. A visitor who hasn't a great many friends will seldom have a really gay time at these parties, but one or two are worth going to just to see the lavish display. The gold plate is brought forth, an extra ballroom is sometimes added to the house, or a tapestry-lined tent is set up, and the gardens are magnificently lighted. An orchestra or two are brought from New York, the house is filled with flowers, and the women all turn out in their most beautiful dresses, resplendent with all the family jewels.

At Saratoga, life centers in the race track and the gambling casino. From the moment when the enthusiast gets up at five in the morning to sit on a rail and clock the horses until time to change for dinner and go to Bradley's for a little gambling, nobody thinks of anything but thoroughbreds. Here it is smart to be well groomed, although sports clothes are the correct costume. Of course, since the season is in August, those smart tweeds that gladden the heart of the keen follower of race meets must be replaced with light-colored sports clothes—something very chic on which to display the indispensable Jockey Club badge.

There isn't much etiquette to a camp in the Adirondacks. The whole day is devoted to sports. No matter how city-bred you are, you can't go very wrong on the matter of clothes for rough, outdoor activities. During the daytime life is pretty well organized. You don't change for dinner and you go to bed early. The same is true of a dude ranch. We went around inquiring right and left about etiquette on the Western plains, and all the information we could get was to take rough, comfortable clothes and riding-togs and not neck the chaps off the cowboys.

At winter resorts of the type where you hope there will be snow on the ground, you live in trousers all day long. Although you can go in for smart color effects, don't lose that certain careless air. Unlike life in summer resorts, that in winter resorts is spent in a hotel or club, because very few people are so fond of the cold, cold air that they take a house for the season on the top of a chilly mountain.

There is some sort of a casino within easy reach of most summer resorts. We're a bit vague as to whether they all operate with the sanction of the law, but nobody seems to bother about it. As long as you're white and twenty-one and have the entrance fee in your pocket, you can get in. Unlike a French casino, where you are apt to spend your whole day and most of the night bathing, lunching, having tea, drinking cocktails, dining, and dancing, as well as gambling, an American one is for gambling only. There is certainly nothing incorrect about being seen at one of these places, and as a girl has to be of age before she can go in, it can scarcely be said that they are corrupters of youth.

At all times your main consideration should be to fit yourself into your background. This is of course true in all places, but never more so than when you are at a resort. You wear the kind of clothes that other people wear; you try to play the games they play and be amused by what amuses them. On the whole, an American resort is no place to go to if you want to be alone or if you need a rest. There is always something doing, if only bridge or backgammon. It's the outdoor woman's real element. No matter how effete you are, you will have to go in for some form of sport, even if the best you can do is go around nine holes in ninety. Whatever activity you choose, on no account let your temper get the better of you. At golf never be the first to drive off unless it is really your honor.

Ask the caddy to tee up your ball or do it yourself, but don't expect one of the men to do it for you; and at the end of the game pay for your own caddy unless you have been playing for his fee. Above all, remember that for all sports low heels are obligatory. Even out sailing you must wear sneakers. We don't quite know why, but it has something to do with the decks.

An Old English Custom

———— ◆ ————

If we have never acquired anything else from the English, we have certainly taken to their week-end habit with ever increasing enthusiasm. Even the smallest and most simple household has its guest-room or has evolved a system of tucking Junior away in some obscure corner from Friday until Monday. The first warm Friday in summer finds us packing our week-end case ready to get out of the city for a rest. (An inveterate visitor continues this all through the winter.) Every Monday we return, worn out and barely able to drag ourselves back to town. But by the next week-end we have recovered, and time has dimmed the memory of the nerve-racking days spent dashing from horse's back to tennis court, to swimming-pool, to late luncheon, to golf course, to three cocktail parties, to dinner, and to the dancing-floor, ending up in a bed with a hump in the middle.

At that, the guest doesn't feel half so weary as the hostess. Probably more hostesses are prostrated on Monday than guests, from the strain of keeping everybody "entertained." The point is that if she didn't struggle to find an amusement for every minute, both she and her guests would pass the time with more enjoyment and less fatigue.

Most of us claim that we'd rather be left to our own devices when visiting. To a certain extent this is true, but it takes a clever hostess to determine where solicitousness ends and neglect begins. The over-zealous type may wear you out, but the indifferent one who goes off in the morning to play tennis, leaving you to shift for yourself the rest of the day, is a bit disconcerting. Of course, if you are in a place where you have lots of friends, this attitude will suit you perfectly, as you will be free to make your own plans, but otherwise it can be extremely dull and rather embarrassing.

Probably the secret of successful entertaining is knowing how to assemble a group of congenial people. This naturally requires a certain genius, but like all genius it is actually a capacity for taking infinite pains. After you've collected the guests, your troubles aren't over, for you have to keep a watchful eye on them and, what's more, be subtle about it. You have to see that they all have plenty of food and drink and that no one is left sitting alone, and you should break up any twosomes where the interest doesn't appear to be mutual. Keep people revolving without their realizing it; this, we admit, takes real talent. Nothing is worse than the officious hostess who is so determined to have her guests enjoy themselves that she runs them ragged. She bustles about, interrupting conversations or separating couples who have just reached the stage where they're making plans for going into the jungle to get away from it all. She herds everybody like sheep, making them go places when they had rather sit still, or forcing backgammon fiends to play bridge.

Think out all the details of menu, service, and amusement well ahead of time and give the necessary orders to the servants. After that think no more about it. If something goes wrong, be philosophical, because it can't be helped. Above all, don't bore your guests with profuse apologies and repetitions of "I can't understand it; this is the first time Cook has ever forgotten to prepare lunch."

At the table, people should be seated with scrupulous care for precedence and sympathy. If two who have never met before are to be next to each other, tactfully give each one an idea of who the other is and an inkling of what interests him. For instance, you may happen to see Lulu White a day or two before the week-end, or you can casually draw her aside on the evening of her arrival, and say: "You're sitting between Jeremiah Penwiper, the author of *My Thirteen Years with a Mummy*, and Henry Whipple, who was at one time Ambassador to Turkey, but now devotes himself entirely to breeding Angora cats." If Lulu doesn't know what to talk about then, you had better stop inviting her to your parties.

Do try to create an atmosphere of hospitality and convey the impression that it is a pleasure to have your friends in the house. Most people had rather not be entertained at all than be given the feeling that their visit is upsetting the entire household and that their hostess can hardly wait for them to go home. Make your wishes clear to your guests before they make any mistakes that might irritate you, and if you have a mania for punctuality, tell them the luncheon and dinner hours as soon as they arrive. By far the pleasantest households to visit are those where everybody is a bit vague—the kind in which the butler announces luncheon, and the hostess says: "Ah, lunch! Let's go for a swim." But, amusing as it is to be irresponsible and eat meals at strange hours, it takes money, so under ordinary circumstances it is better to try to be prompt.

All meals should be arranged for house guests, and they must be included in any parties; but there is no reason why a hostess should worry about them before luncheon time. The afternoons can be planned for either outdoor sports or bridge, according to the tastes of the visitors. Sometimes it may happen that you have been invited to a large and formal dinner before you had planned a house party. If it is impossible to have your guests included in the invitation, all you can do is see to it that they are invited to dine by some friend, or arrange a small dinner at your own house.

The problem of the distribution of rooms more or less solves itself according to the size of the house. Before asking people to double up, be sure that they don't mind, and ask two men, rather than two women, to share a room. Disposing of a husband and wife is not always as simple as it appears on the surface. If there is room enough, don't put them together unless you are sure they have this arrangement at home.

There is no doubt that even in the most palatial homes guest-rooms are seldom comfortable. The beds either sag in the middle or are in need of that housewife's friend, the mattress walker, to tramp down the bulge that keeps the unhappy occupant balancing all night. Beds are placed so that the light from the window shines directly in the sleeper's eyes, and if there is a reading-lamp, it is invariably on the wrong side. You're lucky if the closet boasts one sad little hanger, and the dressing-table is usually so badly lighted that a woman has to use the hit-and-miss system of making up. Perhaps other people have more luck than we do, but the only books we ever find in a guest-room are on the order of hints for the game-hunter in Africa, a history of white slaving in the Argentine, or the second volume of Shakespeare's *Troilus and Cressida*. Only the latest fiction and detective stories should be put on the night table. Magazines seem the obvious choice, but the only copies that ever find their way into a guest-room are a last year's issue of *Time*, or a *Popular Mechanics* discarded by the young son.

Once we stayed in a house where we found a little printed card on our dressing-table. It gave a long breakfast menu which we were to check, and had a space where we were to write in the hour we wanted our tray. But it is not often that one stays in such palatial hotel-like homes. Ordinarily in a large household the maid asks your preferences, and in a small one it is up to the hostess. Come right out with whether you prefer tea or coffee. It is exaggerating politeness to reply: "Oh, anything." This quibbling only wastes time and exasperates the hostess.

Unless you have an extremely small place with only one servant, don't demand that your guests come down for breakfast. Have trays carried up when they ring for them. In the case of very late sleepers who call for breakfast just as the servants are setting the table for luncheon, you need have no qualms about being firm with them. Issue a decree that no breakfast will be served after a certain hour. Late sleepers will then have the choice of eating or sleeping.

Never, on any account, expect or require house guests to accompany you to church. Ask if they want to go, and if they do, you must find some means of transportation for them.

Too many hostesses feel that it is politeness to sit up at night when they are so tired they can do nothing but yawn in their guests' faces. This only means that eventually the rest of the party have to take the hint and go to bed, whether they want to or not. Don't force people into their rooms at night, either by yawns or by direct suggestions. If you are tired, it is far more polite to go quietly off to bed, leaving someone with directions for turning off lights and locking doors—not a feat beyond the ordinary intelligence. The same theory holds for guests. Just because everybody else wants to sit up all night there is no reason for you to try to stick it out if you don't feel that way about the rosy-fingered dawn. Slip away unobtrusively.

The hostess who is against icebox foraging should have a tray of sandwiches and drinks set out in the library or pantry every evening. It is better than having the cold turkey intended for Sunday supper completely demolished.

Only the very, very wealthy can afford to disregard their guests' wires and long-distance telephone calls. It is carrying delicacy too far to refuse to be reimbursed for these items. If possible, leave the matter of collecting bills to the servants. In the case of a long stay they should add up each guest's expenses (including laundry) and present him with the bill before he departs. This system saves you any embarrassment. Of course, it's every visitor's duty to be considerate, use the telephone as little as possible, and insist upon paying for all calls. A host is expected to pay the green fees at a golf club, provide badges for the races, and attend to any other expenses connected with the entertainment of his guests.

In a Strange Bed

—— ◆ ——

Some people always seem to have invitations to visit in friends' houses. They can stay for weeks on end and be asked back again. Obviously, they are the ones who have mastered the difficult art of being a perfect guest. They're always on time for meals, ready on the minute and waiting in the hall when any outing has been planned; they don't make any more demands than necessary on the servants, and they tip generously before leaving.

It's up to you to get some idea of what is going on over the week-end so that you can bring the right clothes. The habitual borrower is never popular and at no time less so than over a week-end when the whole party is in an uproar searching for the necessary tennis rackets, golf sticks, and riding-clothes. Be sure you have everything you need, but don't frighten your hostess to death by arriving with a truck-load of suitcases. And certainly never appear with a dog, no matter how large or small, or how housebroken you consider him.

If you can't move without Marie, warn your hostess that you are bringing her with you. Only very big houses have quarters for visiting maids and valets. If there isn't room for your treasure in the house, arrangements can be made to put her up in a neighboring hotel. Naturally, you pay the bill.

Arrive with your clothes in perfect order so that the maid will not have to spend a whole day washing out your stockings and pressing your frocks. Few suitcases are so well packed that something doesn't need pressing, but always tell the maid in the morning what you're wearing for dinner, so that she will have plenty of time in which to get it ready. Don't start ringing wildly for her five minutes before dinner.

Under no circumstances give an independent order to another person's servant. And if you go often to a house, greet the servants by name when you arrive and thank them before leaving. In fact, try to be pleasant. Tip everybody who has served you. It is an unpleasant custom, but one which prevails in most parts of the world. The size of your tip depends upon your purse and the amount of special attention you have demanded.

No book of etiquette is complete without its list of "dont's," so we are going to get all of them out of our system right now. Here are some for the house guest: Don't drive your host's car around the countryside so furiously that it will have to be put up for minor or serious repairs after your departure, and never drive unless you have a license. Don't take such complete possession of a car that nobody else is able to use it. Don't throw towels on the floor or leave intimate bits of wearing apparel around your room to disconcert your host if he happens to be showing off the beauties of his house. Don't write in bed unless you're sure your pen is filled with washable ink. Don't leave the lights blazing when you go down to dinner. Don't leave the bathroom so wet with steam and cluttered with damp towels that nobody can get into it. Don't discuss the shortcomings of your host with other members of the party. Don't get into heated arguments with other guests or any member of your family who happens to be along. Don't flirt with your hostess's husband or best beau, and don't make scenes with the lady who is making a play for your husband.

If yours happens to be a hostess who insists that you appear in the dining-room for breakfast, stagger down with the pleasantest expression you can muster. Nowadays one is seldom expected to arrive fully clothed. Wash your face, comb your hair and fling a dressing-gown over your nighty or pyjamas, and you're ready. If you are permitted to have a tray upstairs, all the other members of the house party may come in and talk to you. Nobody is shocked any more at the sight of pyjamaed youths sitting on a girl's bed, gnawing crusts of toast from her breakfast tray. If you have an evil mind, a modern house-party is no place to take it.

The one time, however, when a girl must lay off the modern touch is when she is visiting the family of a beau; particularly if they've never met her and suspect, as they invariably do, that she has serious intentions towards their son. They will be on the look-out for defects, so be on your very best behavior all the time. Accede to all their wishes, and don't put the son up to disobeying them. If he doesn't want to fall in with some of their arrangements, let him argue the question, but you appear equally pleased with all decisions. Be on time for all meals and try to keep the young man sober. If he persists in going to sleep on the floor of the drawing-room after you return from a dance, quietly but efficiently get him upstairs and into his room, being careful not to set foot in it yourself. There is no plumbing the depths of a mother's thoughts.

In case of an accident or tragedy in a household, leave immediately, unless you can be of some real assistance. If all the servants walk out, it is usually wiser to follow them, unless you are in a very Bohemian home where such upsets are taken calmly.

All the stratagems for getting away from a boring house party are so worn with use that it requires the ingenuity of a criminal to employ them with success. You must be careful not to telephone or telegraph from the house and, in every other way, to cover up your tracks. The whole thing is slightly simplified when you've been visited with a premonition of approaching boredom. You can then evolve some telegraph code for your family. You wire "How is Fido?" and promptly receive a message: "Grandma dying come home immediately."

But when you finally reach home, your first duty is to take up your pen and write a profuse bread-and-butter letter. It is fatal to put it off until the next day, because if you do, it will never get written. If you let it go for more than a week, you will be ashamed to send it. Everybody knows it's an empty form, but hostesses are touchy about it. Even your best friend is apt to go punctilious on you. A thank-you note will be expected even though you were forced to spend the whole week-end shouting into Mrs. Wordy's ear-trumpet, or were the victim of the practical joker of the party, or all your clothes were burned by the small son with pyro-maniac tendencies, or the friendly dog bit you with remarkable shrewdness. The worst indignity does not excuse you from writing a delirious letter thanking your hostess for a *heavenly* week-end.

Pity the Poor Working Girl

———— ◆ ————

The stay-at-home girl with her handwork is so passé that she has lost her place in the general scheme of things. Her rocker and embroidery frame have been replaced by a swivel chair and a typewriter. In her day the quintessence of feminine charm, the one thing that could be counted upon to break a suitor down, was the sight of a pale hand deftly sewing a fine seam. Nowadays if you were to bend your little golden head over fancy-work, you'd be lucky if you called forth only ribald laughter. Whether we like it or not, we have kissed that angle of femininity good-by. If you must be a womanly woman, you have to be more subtle about it.

Woman's invasion of the drinking world is mild

compared to what she has done to the business world, for even the social butterfly has gone the way of the home-body. Both are headed towards an office. A woman with no job is almost as destitute of playmates during the day-time as a man in the same situation. One has to go to work in self-defense. It isn't always a question of money. Some girls use their extra time and energy in charity work. They are the ones who are either intensely interested in helping the poor or feel that a girl with an independent income should not take a paying job. The old, old argument that can never be settled.

With our lives divided into two distinct parts, the business and the social, we have had to arrange our manners into two sets. For instance, it has become a recognized custom for a man to keep his hat on in an elevator of an office building, although he is still expected to remove it in any other type of elevator. And in an office a man never leaps to his feet when a woman enters the room. The greatest evil which has arisen from this new attitude is a woman's apparent inability to shed her business personality at five o'clock. Men, with the glaring exception of stockbrokers, never seem to have this failing. Not only is it bad form to bring your office into the drawing-room; it is usually poor business. Give your mind a chance to refresh itself.

It is not as illogical as it seems to say that a woman gets into the right frame of mind for business by wearing the right kind of clothes. One of those simple terse-looking little navy-blue models with crisp white collar and cuffs will help convert the limpest little flower into an energetic executive. In spite of this, flowing pastel crepe de chines are remarkably prevalent in an office. Since it has become quite correct to wear spectator sports clothes from early morning until dinner-time, there is no possible reason for buying one of those slinky models. They're not only impractical, but untidy—the last way a girl in an office wants to look. Clothes needn't be expensive, but they should always be neat, simple of line, and fresh-looking.

Make-up in moderation has been as accepted in an office as anywhere else. But if you're a girl with exotic leanings, leave off your crimson nail-polish, eye-shadow, false eyelashes, and long ear-rings. Cache your sex-appeal accessories in your pocketbook until after five o'clock. Trashy novelists to the contrary, "that certain something" isn't what gets you on in the business world. Forget your sex in the office—no man can be on the make twenty-four hours a day.

Be impersonal at all times. The more machine-like, especially in a subordinate position, the more efficient you will be.

Control your personal likes and dislikes. This is particularly necessary in a woman executive, as it doesn't help the office morale to grant more privileges to Mary Smith because you happen to prefer her to Sarah Green.

We all know that awful early-morning feeling when it is much, much easier to turn over and go back to sleep than to stagger towards the shower. But once you've made up your mind to become a working girl, you must face the fact that keeping regular hours is three-quarters of the struggle for a successful career. You must make punctuality a habit.

Don't think that by arriving on the stroke of nine and then taking ten minutes to comb your hair and refresh your make-up you are being punctual. Always allow some time to put yourself in order so that you can be ready and at your desk at the official opening hour. When you first come into an office, ask whether you are to be assigned a locker or are merely expected to hang your clothes on the first convenient peg.

Serious Business

———— ◆ ————

It always comes as a surprise to discover how rigid are the social forms in a business office. One imagines that it is all very casual, but it is actually quite the contrary. Introductions are obligatory. It is supposedly up to the head of the department to introduce herself to any new-comer and then present her to her future associates. When, for some reason, you go from one division to another, it is usual to introduce yourself before stating your business. Eventually the employee is supposed to be presented to everyone in the office by some member of her particular department. There is none of this careless smiling and speaking.

Although in time the girls in offices usually end by

addressing each other by their Christian names, it is more correct, and certainly far safer, to stick to "Miss." Even a married woman is usually "Miss" in an office—back again to the impersonal touch. No matter how many times she has been divorced or widowed, it is customary to cling to the name she had when she first started working. Under no circumstances do you address your masculine associates as anything but "Mr." Any social friendship is forgotten as soon as you reach the office. He can be "Jonathan" to you at dinner, but during working hours he should never be anything else but "Mr. Chale."

A girl always ends by doing what she wants to about going out to luncheon or dinner with her boss, but it is actually very poor policy. It immediately puts their relationship on an entirely different basis. Your social standing is of no consequence. Once you are on a man's pay-roll, you're an employee and should conduct yourself accordingly. Actually you show more pride by keeping your own place and insisting on your employer's keeping his. A friendship of long standing naturally puts a different complexion on the matter. But even then it is bad for office discipline to go out too often and particularly to stay out too long. Under any circumstances it is certainly a bad idea to come back from lunch reeking of cocktails.

Should you have to work overtime, take supper money if the company provides it, but don't accept it directly from your boss. Neither should you go to supper with him if he is also working late. It is impossible to be as impersonal across a dinner-table as it is across a desk.

Although in our first chapter we harped on the casualness of life today, we were referring only to the social aspect. This certainly doesn't hold true in an office. No putting your feet up above your head; no draping yourself over desks; no lounging in chairs. Sit up straight and keep your feet on the floor. Inasmuch as the day is supposed to be spent working, you mustn't interrupt the routine by wandering from one desk to another and chatting aimlessly. In most offices smoking is forbidden, but even where there are no stringent rules, it is not customary to smoke at your desk.

You don't write your personal letters during office hours, and except at lunch-time you shouldn't make any personal telephone calls. Nothing makes a worse impression than hanging on the phone gurgling at your boyfriend. Persuade your friends to call you at home except in cases of extreme urgency. The other girls are apt to get tired of answering the telephone for you. And don't expect anybody to go running all over the office looking for you to tell you that you're wanted on the telephone. Unless you're at your desk, you miss your call.

Older employees usually ask the more recent ones to lunch. In this case offer to pay your own share, although they probably intend to take care of the check as a friendly gesture. But after the first time, and when you have made a similar gesture, each person automatically pays for her own lunch.

When a young man comes to call for you at luncheon or closing time, he should be kept in the reception room unless you prefer to keep him waiting on the corner. No matter how anxious you are to see your latest crush, don't go rushing out before five. And, what's more, wait until then to start putting on your hat and repairing your make-up. This last, incidentally, should be done in the dressing-room.

Leaving for the week-end at Friday noon is all right on special occasions, but should hardly become a habit. Not but what you would soon be aware that it was a poor habit to acquire when you found yourself on the street clutching a little pink slip. There is no doubt about it, the life of a working girl is a hard, hard one. But if you've made up your mind to embark upon a career, we can't stop you. All we can give you are the rules.

Hot Footlights

———— ◆ ————

Although the stigma which was once attached to the theatrical profession began to disappear twenty years ago, it was not until ten years later that a girl of any social prominence could venture upon the boards without being disowned by her family and ostracized by her friends. Nowadays some parents may not like the idea of their sweet, innocent offspring having to cope with the hard-boiled and free-spoken theater world, but they can no longer put up any legitimate objections. It is still considered a bit daring to go on the stage, but a girl who chooses this career will find all her friends out in front more thrilled than shocked.

The greatest argument against a society girl going on the

stage is the fact that she hasn't had the necessary training for that life, and that training counts cannot be denied when one realizes that there have been few great or even successful actresses who did not begin as children. And just to be really encouraging we will tell you that after you've passed twenty, it is usually too late to begin.

It is not the kind of career that can be taken up in a half-hearted fashion, and anyone who lacks a genuine talent for acting should not attempt it. There isn't as much glamour behind the footlights as one would think, and it is the hardest kind of work anybody could possibly undertake and certainly the most confining. It takes that strange and unnamable urge to keep one going through all the hard work and disappointments, and unless you intend to stick to it, it's not worth the agony of beginning.

The general rules of conduct backstage are more difficult to define than those for behavior in an office. It's a world of its own and you can only learn the rules by getting into it. Of course punctuality is even more important in the theater than in the business world, but the stage manager will make this more clear to you than we ever could. Leave your personal emotions and your sensitive feelings at home. They will certainly be in your way on the stage. Gallantry is only excess baggage to a director or stage manager. Their idea is to get as much work out of you as possible and they don't go about it in any gentle manner. If you are going to burst into tears every time they raise their voices, you will soon swim your way out of the theater for good.

The impersonal attitude cannot be over-stressed. The theater is a business like any other, and you should reserve your magnetism for the people across the footlights. Unless you are already on a friendly footing with the director, keep "Mistering" him. At no time accept any favors or invitations from him. You have a better chance of keeping your job by pleading a previous engagement than allowing a situation to come to an issue, and being forced to make your position clear. It is supposed to be impossible for a woman to get on in the theater on her acting talents alone, but it has been done. There are only two alternatives—to give in, or have so much talent that you can make your own terms. Coyness certainly won't get you anywhere.

The Hiccupping Fifties

———— ◆ ————

How noble the prohibitionists felt when, through their efforts, the saloon door swung shut for the last time! Youth and American womanhood were saved from the corrupting influence of this cesspool of vice! We can't suppress an ironical snicker when we think that all they succeeded in doing was transporting women from the drawing-room into the speakeasy. When bobbed hair came in and women invaded the barber-shop, men moaned that their last stronghold had been assailed. Little did they realize how soon it would be before their age-old prerogative of stag drinking was to disappear. Never again will they be able to congregate in a bar-room and relax, for even in the event of prohibition repeal men will have to resign themselves to the fact that the old-time saloon, for men only, will never again exist. Once a woman has felt a brass rail under her instep, there can be no more needlepoint footstools for her.

It doesn't seem so long ago that people went around deploring the fact that women went into speakeasies without a male escort. Now the most correct lady walks in and out of her favorite speakeasy with the same unconcern she would display in going to her hairdresser. Of course it all depends upon the tone of the place. There are some that have become the recognized Mecca of smart feminine lunchers, and in these there is no reason to feel uncomfortable while you sit waiting for your companion.

We have often seen groups of charming little gray-haired ladies happily sealed in a speakeasy, giggling over cordials. But in spite of this, dining with another woman in this type of restaurant is not a practice to be generally advocated. It is not that there is anything inherently wrong in it or, for that matter, in meeting your escort in a speakeasy, but somehow you can't help feeling foolish, and it is always annoying to be leered at by some tipsy old satyr.

In the evening when you have a date with a man and you

have any doubts about the type of place you are going to, save yourself any possible embarrassment by refusing to meet him there. Insist that he call for you at your house.

Whether you are with a man or a woman, the chief consideration is to remain as inconspicuous as possible. Raucous laughter, silly screams, and wild gesticulations will immediately draw attention to you, to your companion's intense embarrassment. And besides you'll be accused of being tight whether you are or not. At any point in the game long conversations with the waiters just to show off your knowledge of a foreign language are pretty boring to the bystanders. But a girl who leans over the bar in a heart-to-heart talk with the bar-tender is just plain objectionable. Particularly to her boyfriend.

You, too, probably have your little prejudices; one of ours is the friendly drunk who either sits at the table next to you and enters into the conversation or comes weaving across the room at you. We're just magnets for them. Getting rid of this type of bore is no easy matter. There are two schools of thought on the subject. One contends that if you don't buy him a drink, he just stays on hoping, while the other maintains that if you buy him one drink, he will sit on and on waiting for the next. But one thing we've discovered—if you once permit him to launch on his life history, all is lost. The best thing for a girl to do is to take refuge in the ladies' room and leave her companion to deal with the situation.

Soon the man who can drink and hold his liquor will become extinct—a legendary figure. No longer is drinking an art with Americans; once they drank for the taste, but now they drink only for the effect. The more quick and fatal the liquor, the better they like it. They are either on the wagon or else.

There was once a time when a man who got drunk in a lady's drawing-room was never invited to that house again. If he showed the same lack of control in another home, he ran the risk of having every door closed to him. Now a hostess who insists that all her guests remain sober would find that she was giving parties to a chosen few, and very dull ones at that. She takes it for granted that the majority of her guests will be wavering before the evening is over. It may seem sad, but it is certainly true that the conversations the day after a successful party are invariably on the order of: "Were you there when Jack fell off the chandelier?—*too* funny! I thought I'd die laughing," or: "Did you see Tom upping into the umbrella-stand? Old Mr. McCandless arrived too late to rescue his umbrella and was perfectly furious."

Cocktail parties have become the line of least resistance in entertaining. They are convenient for the person who must get fifty or sixty people off the list of obligations and prefers to do it at one fell swoop, saving money at the same time. It certainly isn't much trouble; all you need is a case of synthetic gin and a tin of anchovy paste. The greater the number of the guests, the smaller and more airless the room, the stronger the gin, the more successful the party. But if you give one, you must be prepared to have your friends on your hands until two in the morning, as they will invariably forget their dinner engagements and stay on until the last shakerful is emptied.

Our Plastered Friends

———◆———

When our mothers came out, learning to handle a drunk was not an essential part of a debutante's education. Now every girl has to be capable not only of shifting for herself, but, more often than not, of looking out for her escort as well. However, it must be confessed that the bad manners and drunkenness of men are largely due to the fact that girls are much too tolerant. They are willing to put up with anything rather than run the risk of losing a beau. Of course if they themselves drink, they are only too delighted to have their companions reach the point where they don't know what goes on. A great many people have come to believe in the single moral standard, but few have been converted to a single drinking standard. A drunken woman is still looked upon with disgust and she is certainly more objectionable than a drunken man. Liquor generally hits her in one of three ways—she gets boisterous and wants to play games, or she gets maudlin, or, more often, she grows desperately amorous. Whatever the effect, she is dangerous. Her games are apt to be rough, her tears collar-wilting, and her love-making too public and too earnest for fun.

One damsel who heard about our advice for handling a drunk grew hoity-toity. "*My* escorts never get tight," she told us, implying that she moved in a circle in which such things didn't happen. Strange. The only way we can figure it out is that she is too dumb to know when a man is slightly the worse for wear. Or she just goes out with sissies.

If you're going out very often, you might as well be prepared to think quickly and be ready to exercise your ingenuity at any time. You may be called upon to do anything from catching the bottles that your escort, in his exuberance, may chance to throw, to burrowing in the sawdust for him. It all demands presence of mind, poise, and resourcefulness. Useful qualities, but, alas, only acquired with experience. A drunken man's imagination is so fantastic that it is a bit difficult to anticipate his actions. Drunks can be divided into about ten standard types. There are more, of course, but actually they are only variations of these ten:

The *hilarious* is the pleasantest by far. He may embarrass you a bit by getting very noisy, or by being overwhelmed with a desire to sing; but the laughter of the people around you is good-humored, and the queer things he will think up to do will often be irresistibly funny. If you want to enjoy yourself, it is up to you to get into the spirit of the thing.

The *lachrymose* decides that life is a sad, sad business, that he hasn't a friend in the world, and that nobody loves him. He is apt to burst into tears at the slightest provocation, and any argument which attempts to persuade him that he is loved by the entire world is hopeless and only leads to endless discussion.

The *loquacious* is about the most boring of all. He gets you at his mercy and either tells endless, rambling stories or repeats the same one over and over again. Once he gets started, it is hopeless to divert him. Don't try to stop him. Just sit and think of something else, but keep a look of rapt attention on your face. When he looks as though he expected a reply, merely nod, and that will satisfy him.

The *taciturn,* on the other hand, may not provide a very amusing evening, but he is certainly less annoying than the talkative kind. Don't feel called upon to fill in the long silences. Relax and make this your evening of rest.

The *argumentative* disagrees with you every time you enter into the conversation. No matter what you say, he flatly contradicts you. But it is in restaurants that he gets particularly obnoxious. He complains loudly about the food. "I ordered whitebait, and these look like whales," he will repeat over and over until everybody at the table, not to say in the restaurant, feels like choking him. Don't attempt to placate him or make any reply. Pay no attention to him and go on with your dinner. When, as a last crowning touch, he decides he has been gypped on the check, grab your powder-puff and flee to the ladies' room, where you can stay until the row has been settled and it is time to go home.

The *magisterial* is irritating because he is so overbearing. Of course if you can preserve your sense of humor, his sweeping gestures, lofty manners, and five-syllable words, spoken with such authority, cannot help amusing you.

The *belligerent* who wants to fight every man in sight is very difficult to handle, since, sooner or later, he is bound to find somebody who is just as tight as he is and who will be willing to take up the challenge. If you can't prevail on him to go home, and if flight is impossible, try to make him forget his grievances, or keep out of the way. When the fur does begin to fly, *never* interfere.

The *vomitous,* who reacts to liquor as he would to a rough sea, requires a firm touch. Send him home at the first indication of that uncertain feeling or have him led to the nearest bathroom and leave him there. Then take your mad money and go home.

The *sentimental* goes into reveries about sweet Mabel, the love of his adolescent years, or grows misty-eyed at the mention of his college pal, Ben Hicks, a prince among men, with a voice that is clear and true as he is, which is diamond-true. It is unwise, to say the least, to remind him that his noble Ben beats his wife, for you will never be able to survive the torrent of vindication you will have called forth. Keep silent and look sympathetic.

The *amorous* is by far the hardest to control and certainly the most prevalent. If you suspect that you are out with the erotic type, keep him in a crowd. And if this is impossible, ply him with liquor until he gets beyond the dangerous stage.

When out with a plastered friend, control your feelings and on no account lose your temper. Let go the next day; the angrier you get, the better; but at the time fight down any desire you may have to give him a piece of your mind. It only leads to a scene and makes no impression. Remain calm and try to get him to go home, but under no circumstances let him suspect you think he is tight. There is nothing that will infuriate him like a just suspicion of his condition. Agree with everything he says, as nine times out of ten he will forget it five seconds later. If you argue with him, you fix the idea in his mind. If he wants to take the orchestra away with him, be thrilled. If he develops a craving to play the saxophone, *love* saxophones and don't mention the merits of the tuba. If he takes a dislike to a stranger across the room and decides he wants to punch him, agree that the man has an ugly face, but try to shift the conversation to another subject, and if the fight seems unavoidable, leave by the nearest exit.

A cold shower is undoubtedly one of the most effective means of sobering a person, but in a restaurant or speakeasy you can't very well resort to this time-honored remedy. The only hope of sobering your companion a bit is to persuade him that what he most wants is a cup of black coffee. Coffee with milk or cream in it is of no use for this purpose, and to let him drink water is fatal.

When your escort passes out in a public place, waste no time worrying over him. Get up and leave quickly; take a taxi and go home. He will find his way home somehow when he comes to or has been thrown out by the management. If you are fond of the young man and don't wish him to get into too much trouble, you might take his money and other valuables before departing, leaving him only taxi fare. If you do this, he won't be able to get into any further mischief when he recovers.

When your companion passes out in a taxi, get out at your own house, give the driver the young man's address, and think no more about him. Of course, if you should be very annoyed, you might tell the driver to take the lad to Yonkers or some obscure spot in Brooklyn. The trouble and expense that this will cause him should amply satisfy your desire for revenge.

Never, never go out at night without a few pennies in your purse; call it "mad money" or what you like, it will pay for your taxi home if the need should arise.

Learn to drive a car whether you own one or not. The day will surely come when you will have to take the wheel or run the risk of crashing against a tree with a youth whose drinks have affected his vision. In fact, if you take our advice, you will carry caution to the extent of never getting into a car with a man you know is drunk. Even if you are at a friend's house in the country and you suddenly realize that your young man has reached this stage, don't go home with him. Spend the night where you are, no matter how embarrassing it may be. After all, plastic surgery is pretty expensive.

Going home in a taxi with an inebriate also has its perils. Not only is your virtue at stake, but you are sure to get your newest Chanel torn to ribbons. However unromantic our view-point, you must admit it is certainly practical.